fagih@hotmail.com

GAZELLES AND OTHER PLAYS

Kegan Paul proudly introduces a collection of five works intended for the stage - translated from their original Arabic into English. *Gazelles*, the central play within the book, contains many of Fagih's common themes. The story of Jabar, a Bedouin desert guide, and two Westerners, Victor and Helena, the play examines the relationships between Eastern and Western cultures. All the plays published in this collection have already appeared in theatre production. Filled with the same imagery and poetic fancy Fagih's prose are renowned for, *Gazelles and Other Plays* will appeal to theatre aficionados and general readers alike.

GAZELLES AND OTHER PLAYS

AHMED FAGIH

KEGAN PAUL INTERNATIONAL
London and New York

First Published in 2000 by
Kegan Paul International Limited
UK: P.O. Box 256, London WC1B 3SW, England
Tel: 020 7580 5511   Fax: 020 7436 0899
E-mail: books@keganpaul.com
Internet: http://www.keganpaul.com
USA: 61 West 62nd Street, New York, NY 10023
Tel: (212) 459 0600   Fax: (212) 259 3678
Internet: http://www.columbia.edu/cu/cup

Distributed by

John Wiley & Sons
Southern Cross Trading Estate
1 Oldlands Way, Bognor Regis
West Sussex, PO22 9SA, England
Tel: (01243) 779 777   Fax: (01243) 820 250
E-mail: cs-books@wiley.co.uk

Columbia University Press
61 West 62nd Street, New York, NY 10023
Tel: (212) 459 0600   Fax: (212) 259 3678
Internet: http://www.columbia.edu/cu/cup

Printed in Great Britain, Pear Tree Press

ISBN: 0-7103-0633-4

British Library Cataloguing in Publication Data
Applied For

Library of Congress Cataloging-in-Publication Data
Applied For

Gazelles and other plays

Contents

ACT ONE

JABER   *a bedouin from the Sahara. In his fifties. Stockily built, wearing Sahara dress, acting as a guide on the journey.*

VICTOR   *an engineer in his fifties, with an American company, prospecting for oil in the Kingdom. Victor is British, has a flat in London but works mostly in an underground laboratory in the Kingdom. He has invited Helena to accompany him on a trip into the desert to hunt gazelles.*

HELENA   *a young Englishwoman in her twenties. She works for a building society in London. She has lived in Lancashire and West Yorkshire.*

(The desert. Just before sunrise. The horizon glows.

A Land Rover. Scattered around it, pots and pans, collapsing chairs, a table, the remains of a meal.

Stage right, an empty bed with a hunting rifle next to it.

Stage left, a tent for two in which VICTOR and HELENA lie in bed. They are struggling under the covers. A radio stands by the bed, and we see, through the open flaps of the tent, HELENA'S hand come out to switch on the radio. VICTOR'S hand emerges and switches it off. And so on. The radio manages to give out sporadic news items.)

RADIO   New steps have been ... meanwhile in Washington ... Eyeball to eyeball confrontation ... No surrender to blackmail ...

(Radio is switched off by VICTOR.

HELENA pushes VICTOR off her. She hides under the

1

bed covers.)

HELENA   Have you gone daft?

VICTOR   That's right.

HELENA   It's morning and stuff.

VICTOR   Right.

HELENA   Well, the bedouin will see us.

VICTOR   He thinks we're married. Let me ... come on. Give it a go.

HELENA   Don't be dopey. Lots and lots and lots and lots more romantic nights in the desert.
(She pushes him, laughing, so he falls out of bed.)

(VICTOR pulls on his trousers and wraps himself in a blanket to protect himself from the cold of the desert. HELENA leaps out of bed and puts on her Safari clothes. She comes out of the tent, goes to the watercan in the back of the Land Rover, splashes water on her face and begins to comb her hair, gazing in astonishment at the horizon glowing red with the sunrise.)

HELENA   Dawn in the desert. Magnificent. Like a postcard. And me in the middle of the photo. *(Splashes more water on her face)*. Ouch, it's like mashed ice. Why don't they fit these chariots with running hot and cold?

VICTOR   *(brushing his teeth, ignoring the view)* Where's Jaber?

HELENA   *(She looks around)* Last time I looked he was lighting a fire for my Typhoo. Now he's vanished. Hey, he was really weird last night with that snake. First he held it like a baby sparrow with a bad wing. Then he cut with his knife, sliced off its head, boiled it up and gulped it down. Ugh. And then he said: 'Among all the delights of the desert, this is my favourite repast.'

2

I'll be telling my great-grandchildren that story, but they won't believe it. Basically, even for a guide, that man is odd. Who recommended him?

VICTOR   Bedouins tend to believe the non-toxic parts of snakes are good medicine, stomach-wise. I'd eat a raw snake if it'd snap me out of the dodgy spell that hit me yesterday. It's because I work underground all day. Away from the light. Down in that laboratory. When you come out the sun smacks you round the head. Look, Helena, I'm sorry. Really sorry. Must have been dead frustrating for you. Awful.

HELENA   Don't worry, Victor. That's nothing. First time together, first night in the desert. You won't need a snake supper.

(VICTOR begins to shave. HELENA sits with her handbag beside her and becomes absorbed in putting on her make-up.)

I was scared.

VICTOR   I'm sorry, I didn't mean –

HELENA   Not by you. By the wolves. When the wolves started howling. Where's my bloody eyebrow pencil? Why do they make 'em so easy to lose? They didn't stop howling all night. Choir practice. Or an all-night sitting of the House of Wolverines. And I thought: wish I could understand Wolfish. Wonder what they were on about. Bet it wasn't inflation or the energy crisis or the dollar going up and down and up. I'm perfectly well aware that this kind of make-up's totally useless in the desert sun. But it's all I've brought. I forgot to buy my Sahara beauty kit. Nearly forgot my face, too. That howling. *(She imitates it)* Howling in harmony. *(VICTOR joins in)* Yes. It was just beside us and it was all around us, all over us, like a great dome of howling. A wolfskin dome. That guide of yours was getting all poetic: 'The desert belongs to the gazelles' – but I think the wolves had

3

'em for breakfast. He could see I was scared. By the howling. So he said: 'Don't be frightened. The howling of wolves is like the light of the stars. They both travel a long way.' A long way! And next minute a wolf comes strutting along and squats down for a crap right by the Land Rover. Wouldn't even shift till you fired your rifle. I was in a right panic. So when something jumped into bed on top of me I thought it was a wolf.

VICTOR   It was me. I love you. You're a gazelle. Did I tell you?

HELENA   You promised me gazelles. You said you'd show me real gazelles.

VICTOR   That's what we're here for. To see the gazelles.

HELENA   What's so special about them?

VICTOR   We won't know that till we see them. *(VICTOR carries on shaving)*

HELENA   Gazelles. My dreams were full of gazelles. I looked into one of my dreams, you know, like looking down into a pool. And I saw myself walking between two young gazelles, my hands on the back of their necks and I was leading them home. Then it was another dream. And there was a great mob of gazelles chasing me, like hooligans, like they wanted to hurt me with their horn things.

VICTOR   And didn't I feature in any of your dreams?

HELENA   What I'd really love is a good old wallow in a foaming hot bath full of pink chemicals. I'll send a postcard to my bathroom – wish you were here. I feel little and lost without four walls and a ceiling. Oh, all right, it's a unique experience. I expect the desert's going to release something really surprising that's been locked up in me. Ooch! I've never seen anyone shave with a razor like that. I thought everyone'd gone electric.

VICTOR   I have to use a blade. Got that kind of a face. Maybe my face is behind the times. Ouch, that hurt, my face must be listening to us. Look, you can't waltz into the middle of the desert and expect bath, shower, bidet and rubber duck. Great thing is to forget the city, wipe it out of your mind. Just take what the desert has to offer. Gratefully. The desert is different. Different. We spend our days moving from one box to another: from the flat box into the car box into the office box, down to the lab box, out to the restaurant box, back to the lab box, out to the car box, back to the flat box, close the lid, goodnight. But a few days in the desert can scrub out of our brain cells all the dust and dirt from those boxes. All that gentle, phosphorescent dust which drifts in through our pores, and piles up in corners of our brains as the days and the years go by. They clog up our minds, they won't work properly. All you can do is climb out of our boxes and stand out in the open.

HELENA   That's why I'm here, kid.

(Kneels and declaims theatrically)

Oh! Mighty Desert!
Oh! Gigantic boundless ocean without water!
Oh! Wonderful new cities of steel and glass which have not yet been built!
Oh! Jungle without trees!
Oh! Mighty Desert!
Oh! You amazing letter A in the alphabet of the universe!
Oh! You enormous empty origin of everything!
I have come to hide myself in you!

(She gets up, laughing, and resumes her normal tone of voice)

I better write that in my diary before I forget it.

(She dances over to the Land Rover while VICTOR

applauds her performance admiringly)

VICTOR   I didn't know you were a poet.

HELENA   I'm an escaped convict. From an office prison, with its
            files and phone calls and photo-copying – all that can
            kill you. And that letter. That's the worst. I'm really
            running away from the ghost of that letter.

VICTOR   What letter? Who sent it you?

            *(VICTOR has finished shaving and is slapping on
            after-shave lotion. Then he begins to do his morning
            exercises)*

HELENA   You're part of the Lucky Gang. You know, people
            who've got jobs which let them be creative and
            inventive and that. You couldn't understand the
            trudging drudgery of somebody who spends her life
            slaving over a hot IBM?

VICTOR   Some hard luck story. The world depends on beautiful
            secretaries. Corporations and governments would
            collapse without them.

HELENA   *(still writing in her diary)* 'I have come to hide myself
            in you.' That letter. There's only one letter. Every day
            I sit up when the sun sits up. When he packs it in, so
            do I. The words I type are like little ropes which
            tangle round me and bind me down like Gulliver in
            Lilliput. Or they're a swamp of tar and I'm sinking
            down and when the tar reaches my neck I scream –
            and that means it's one o'clock. Out to the canteen for
            a salad or a sandwich, then back to face the machine
            which eats me, and the tar of boredom's nearly
            covering my face when it's time to say goodbye
            bloody office. One more day without actually
            drowning in tar!

            *(She throws her diary on to the table and pretends to
            type)*

6

'Dear Mr So-and-so, We are pleased to inform you that your request for a loan to cover the purchase of number whateveritis, Hellfire Avenue, Satanstown has been approved by the committee' *(snatches imaginary paper out of typewriter, inserts new page)*. Two carbons, change paper. 'Dear Mr So-and-so, We are pleased to inform you' – Bugger Mr So-and-so and his family and the loan on the house and that typewriter. I bash out that message a million times a day and it's always the same except sometimes we are sorry to inform you that the committee has not approved. What I want to do is set my machine to print out one reply, the same reply for every single Mr So-and-so: 'Dear Mr So-and-so, Why throw away your cash on an ugly little house in a nasty little town? A pigsty in the country would be healthier and a ball and chain would be more fun. Love and kisses from all of us at the Kirkby Lonsdale Building Society.' Oh, I get throttled with rage, really throttled. By the time I've written to the thirtieth Mr So-and-so I'm ready to swallow dive out the office window, nine floors down and hope to zap the boss's Jag. That's what I was daydreaming when Dogface plonked your note on my desk 'Sweet Helena, I'm going to the Sahara to hunt gazelles. Please come and help me. Love, Victor.' I scrunched up my letter to Mr So-and-so number thirty, switched off my typer, booked an emergency compassionate leave, bought my ticket, collected my visa and flew out to you. I hated houses, hated cities, I was full of a dream of the great desert. I'd better take some snaps now I'm here.

(She takes her camera from the car and begins to take pictures)

Laughing's the opposite of crying. Dancing and singing are the opposite of unhappiness. Pleasure's the opposite of pain, light's the opposite of darkness. Day – night. Speech – silence. Love – hate. Health – sickness. Freedom – slavery. Life – death. And it just seemed to me that desert is the opposite of city.

VICTOR   I was so happy when you phoned up and said yes.

HELENA   Took you by surprise?

VICTOR   You answered so quickly. Shall I smile?

(She takes a picture of him)

HELENA   You don't have to smile. You know the world is packed full of people. Doesn't that boggle your mind a bit? It boggles mine. Me in the desert. Alone in the universe. The world belongs to me. I feel as if we've come on a long journey through space and we'd just landed on earth. Victor. It's the dawn of history. My name's Eve. Who are you?

VICTOR   Adam.

JABER   *(offstage)* Don't forget the serpent. May God forgive you.

(JABER comes in and puts breakfast in front of them with a pair of binoculars – tea and bread)

JABER   Your breakfast is served.

VICTOR   You interrupted Helena.

(VICTOR starts to eat with HELENA)

JABER   Why did you not go and get warm?

VICTOR   Why light the fire so far from our tent?

JABER   Not too near the car and the petrol cans.

HELENA   Has it gone out yet?

JABER   It won't go out till I put it out.

HELENA   I'll go and have a little warm-up. Take a photo of me by the fire. Oh no! The milk's gone off.

8

(HELENA goes offstage to the fire)

JABER   Personally, I only drink sour milk.

(JABER waits, then takes a photo of HELENA)
(to VICTOR) You were talking of something the desert has to offer.

VICTOR   You've got good reception.

JABER   Did you mean oil?

VICTOR   No, I meant something glorious. Something eternal.

JABER   Oil is not eternal. And it doesn't smell glorious. But where would we be without it? And where would this desert be? The desert will never forget how much it owes to people like yourself. You studied its depths and revealed its minerals so that, at last, the desert can be useful. A man from our village used to come hunting with me. In those days he was poorer than me. But now he's an oil sheikh with luxury villas all around the world. He's just like me really, except that he has a millionaire son married to the daughter of one of our rulers. How could he forget what he owes you and your oil company.

VICTOR   Let the oil sheikhs speak for themselves. Listen, Jaber, why didn't you sleep by the Land Rover?

JABER   I didn't want to crowd you. Why all sleep in one bedroom when the desert is filled with bedrooms? *(With a touch of sarcasm)* Anyway, between you and me, I like to watch things from a distance.

VICTOR   You were watching us? You dirty old guide. Are you from the Sun?

JABER   I don't object to our changing places, Mr. Victor.

VICTOR   That's enough! She's my wife.

JABER   We all know you're not married. But that doesn't stop

9

me envying you, Mr. Victor.

VICTOR   Why?

JABER   Two reasons. You've been smart enough to pretend that she's your wife so you can travel around with her freely. And when you chose her, you chose a gazelle. She makes the gazelles of the desert look clumsy-footed and bleary-eyed. She's the ideal age, too. You know what we say in the desert? There's only one way for an old man to get back his youth. This is the prescription: marry a woman in her twenties. That's what we all do, when we start to totter a little. One of the Sheikhs in our tribe felt himself ageing. He couldn't walk, he couldn't even stand. So he married a young woman of 18. He was on the large side, and on the wedding night it took four men, working as a team, to place him on top of his bride. Next morning he was with the kids in the market-place. Take my advice: let your body roll around with that young body of hers, let them play together. Make her sometimes your couch and sometimes your coverlet. Take her by surprise. Let her lie on you and infuse you with the heat of her body till you hear the sweat pouring off you. And every little sickness will fly out of your body. That's our treatment.

VICTOR   I'd prefer you to keep your primeval holistic theories to yourself. Why don't you believe she's my wife? I just didn't think she was worthy to live in your wonderful kingdom of sand and grit. And, since I couldn't leave my important job for long enough to visit England, she came to me. And because she wanted two days' worth of desert, here she is.

JABER   Not a bad story. But look, we're companions on a journey. Why not make me your friend?

VICTOR   Because you're not my friend. And whether I'm married to Helena or not married to Helena only matters to me and Helena.

JABER	And me.
VICTOR	How so?

(HELENA comes in and places her empty teacup on the tray)

HELENA	Oh Victor, do drop all that flapdooodle about us being married. What' s the point?
VICTOR	Helena, we're not on Brighton beach.
HELENA	I'm with you.
VICTOR	We're in the Kingdom.
HELENA	Still here.
VICTOR	And people round here don't recognise any male-female relationship outside marriage. They call it prostitution.
HELENA	Well, I haven't been paid.
VICTOR	Or fornication.
HELENA	Well, I haven't – no comment.
VICTOR	To get you a visa I had to write affidavits for the Police and the Company and the Department of Immigration and even then the Morals Squad were dubious. They followed us all around town –
HELENA	The ones with dark glasses and flares –
VICTOR	The only thing that stopped them was the desert. They could stick us in jail and then throw us out of the country.
HELENA	Couldn't be that bad.
VICTOR	Could be much worse. You tell her, Jaber.

JABER	Don't worry, Helena. He says you're his wife. But that doesn't commit you to anything. It just protects you from the pack of wolves who'd come howling after you if they knew you were a husbandless, family-free woman travelling on her own through the desert.
HELENA	I don't get it.
JABER	*(To VICTOR)* Don't give me that look. I won't tell anyone that you and her are ...
VICTOR	*(To HELENA)* OK, let's drop it.
JABER	If you have finished your breakfast perhaps you would like to start. There is a herd of gazelles grazing only an hour from here.
VICTOR	Gazelles? How d'you know?
JABER	I was beyond that ridge keeping watch for them just now.
VICTOR	Helena! Gazelles. Let's move.
HELENA	What's the rush? They've been here for centuries.
VICTOR	Well done, Jaber. *(VICTOR jumps in the Land Rover)*
HELENA	I can't start the day without my music. *(Takes out her portable radio and fiddles with it to find music.)*
VICTOR	*(To Land Rover):* Come on! It won't start.
HELENA	Over here, Jaber. Dancing lesson!
JABER	*(Laughing)* I've never danced. Not a step. Never even seen a night-club.
HELENA	A night-club's like a dungeon at rush-hour. The men get pissed at the bar and the women go to the lavatory in pairs. And there's stupid traffic lights flashing

away.

JABER   What?

VICTOR   Won't bloody start.

HELENA   They always start in the end. *(To JABER)* Most of the
men dance like camels but they smell worse. And the
bouncers are built like pyramids.

Oh sorry. Most of the men dance like camels but they
smell worse. And the bouncers are built like pyramids.

JABER   Is there music?

HELENA   No, there is a noise called disco. Sounds like a bunch
of eunuchs yelling for help from the top of an oil
derrick. You haven't missed much.

VICTOR   Bloody hell. *(Jumps out of Land Rover, opens front)*

JABER   But I've missed the pleasure of holding a young
woman close, me loving her and her loving me back.
You see, when I reached the age of love I never knew
love, or music, or dancing. It was like sitting for year
after year with a hot coal in my hand. The desert stole
all those joys away from me.

HELENA   You talk like a child who's had a toy pinched.

VICTOR   Could be dirty plugs. *(Gets to work with a cloth)*

JABER   I never had a toy. When people are waiting to be born
they should be asked where they want to spend their
lives. I'd have chosen a great city like yours. And I'd
only visit the desert as a tourist. Like Victor. And I'd
invite you.

HELENA   I'd have chosen the desert. I could have been your
guide. You don't want the city. Bricks and mortar,
bricks and mortar, wherever you go the walls close in
around you, walls piled on top of each other, bricks

13

and mortar – You feel that your eyes are made of bricks, your heart is made of bricks, you've got a brickhead, brick body, brick feet. Towers of steel and concrete and glass rise up everywhere and wipe out the horizon and the sun and the colours of the clouds and the deeps of the sky. It's like we'd swapped our space in the universe for a million cages built with bricks and mortar.

(VICTOR back in Land Rover – won't start)

JABER   Give me your walls and take my desert. Perhaps I could travel back to my empty childhood and find it suddenly filled with toy cars, bright roundabouts, cartoon films, new clothes, birthday parties and boxes of chocolates.

VICTOR   Toy cars. That's what I've got here.

HELENA   But Jaber, I didn't eat your chocolates. Don't look so sorry for yourself. What was your school like?

JABER   It was one dark room with a blind sheikh and his stick. We read the Quran there for two years. That was education in my village. The only good things were the pictures on the walls. I think they must have been posters from the Department of Health. They showed wonderful children. Dressed in new clothes, marvellous clothes. Beautiful features, rosy cheeks, carefully combed and glossy hair, wide bright eyes. They smiled down at me with their glittering teeth. Their world was spotless and shining, a world bursting with health and beauty. And then I'd look around me. Real school children. Ragged old clothes. Skinny little bodies. Flies hovering around their eyes, their nose and their mouths, sucking at their snot and their spittle. And I hated them all.

I wasn't any brighter or cleaner than the worst of them, but I could still curse fate for putting me among them. One day I looked up to the children in the pictures and saw them looking down at me. I realised that they'd chosen me to be their friend. I was so happy. The dingy room disappeared and the blind sheikh waving his devilish stick vanished, and so did all of those little faces which packed the room around me like a heap of rusty old tins. From then on I greeted the picture children every morning. I gave them beautiful names like the names in our school books. I never left my classroom without saying goodbye to them. One day perhaps they would climb out of their pictures and play.

HELENA   And what do you feel about those picture children now? Do you hate them for what they had and what you never had?

JABER   Oh no. I'm grateful to them. They gave me the only happy memories of my children. If I hadn't met them in that room, my mind would have been destroyed.

HELENA   *(going towards him and taking both his hands)* Any friend of theirs is a friend of mine.

VICTOR   Still won't start.

HELENA   Sand in the carburettor?

VICTOR   D'you know about cars?

HELENA   I know they get sand in the carburettor.

VICTOR   Ah. *(He goes back to working on the engine).*

JABER   Is it going to work?

VICTOR   Of course it's going to work.

HELENA   That's the spirit. Come on Jaber, let's dance! I'll teach you how the city dances. You teach me how the desert dances.

           (She pulls him forward to dance. He resists a little, then begins to dance with her, stumbling along.

15

HELENA tries to teach him to dance)

Right foot first. Then the left. Get your feet to follow
the beat. Like I do. Watch me. Follow me.

*(He tries to follow her but starts dancing in his own
way, excited, powerful but ignoring the rhythm of the
music. By mistake he treads on her foot. She yells. He
stops dancing. She laughs. He laughs too)*

You dance like a crocodile.

JABER   I accept that as a compliment since it comes from such
             a gracious lady as yourself.

             (The music stops. Huge applause)

RADIO   And that's where we leave Wembley Arena, where
             Doberman's Platoon are receiving a standing ovation
             – as usual.

             *(Serious march music strikes up – a second radio
             voice, very authoritative, comes in)*

SECOND
RADIO
VOICE   World Perspectives. *(Music fades)* This week our team
             reports on and examines the latest developments in the
             global energy crisis. Our guests in the studio include
             the Minister and Shadow Minister for Energy, a panel
             of leading economists and businessmen with a satellite
             link-up to their counterparts in New York and a
             representative of the Third World. We begin -

HELENA   Music, give me music.

             (HELENA turns the dial to other stations)

RADIO   *(Actory voice)* L'oiseau chant avec ses doights – trois
             fois … *(burst of Arabic)* … *(comic's voice)* So my old
             woman said to me: 'I don't know, but I put what was
             left in your sandwiches.' *(roar of laughter)* …

16

VICTOR   *(Back in driver's seat – won't start)* Oh damn it to hell!

HELENA   Music!

RADIO   *(Huge burst of music from Wagner's The Ring. She switches it off).*

HELENA   Stupid radio. Tell me about your gracious lady.

JABER   I have no gracious lady. Just a wife.

HELENA   If that's a joke I think you ought to build a sphinx on top of it. One wife? What a comedown! You're a free spirit of the desert. You're meant to marry twenty, fifty, a hundred women.

JABER   That was our ancestors, Miss Helena.

HELENA   Real men.

JABER   Yes, powerful, tall and domineering. They darkened the face of the desert with their camels and their stallions. Their tents were numberless. One man would have a hundred or two hundred women in his household. Sometimes a thousand or two thousand for a prince or a king. But then along came new generations of feeble little men with weak appetites. They couldn't rise to the standards of their glorious ancestors. And a strange law crept in, I don't know how, but it stopped a man from keeping more than one wife. It seemed like the end of the world. But, Allah be praised, there was no law against a man separating from his wife. So all we could do was marry them one at a time, keep them for a year or two, then divorce one wife and marry another.

HELENA   That's what we do with cars. What about the poor woman you married just so you could divorce her?

JABER   She doesn't mind – she goes out and marries another

17

man. In our villages we celebrate weddings as often as you throw tea parties.

HELENA   I have never thrown a tea party in my life.

JABER   That's why you're not married.

HELENA   Tell me Jaber, have you ever got a divorce so you could marry another woman?

JABER   Of course. Eleven women. Most of them, by Allah, were virgins.

HELENA   Eleven. Let me take a photo!

VICTOR   I'm going off for a crap.

JABER   Only eleven. Where I come from I'm regarded as a bachelor. You're not allowed to meet your bride before the wedding. You don't even see her. So the only way you can find out about her is to marry her. Then if you don't like her, you divorce her so you can marry someone else. And so on and so on till you find the right person and then you decide to be partners for life.

HELENA   Smile, please! *(adjusts camera)* That's a great way to get to know people. And after all your eleven marriages, have you finally found your life partner? Smile!

JABER   I had a little patch of land. I sowed it with wheat every winter. When summer came and the wheat ripened I cut it down and hauled it off to market. With the money I earned I'd order a wedding party. But times have changed. My children have multiplied. They're like ants, all over the house. Life is more complicated. There are more demands on me. My crops won't keep my family for more than a month or two. On top of that I'm getting older and I'm fed up with being a guide. The last woman fate sent me is satisfactory, oh, but to be honest: if Mr Victor paid me proper wages

18

I'd go off and marry another virgin straight away and with the permission of Allah she would cure the weakness I feel crawling in my arms and legs. It's extraordinary that a man of Victor's age isn't married. In my village, when a man's over twenty, the less he's married, the more he's talked about. A man who's not married at all – what does he do with his virility? But a man of fifty, still not married, what about him?

HELENA   He's internationally famous.

JABER   For being unmarried?

HELENA   No, for his work in oil research. He might never have done that if he'd been bothered with a house and wife and kids.

JABER   But what's the use of being internationally famous? At the end of every day he finds his home as empty as a lizard's hole in the desert.

HELENA   You don't want to understand. It's perfectly normal. Some people choose not to marry. I'm never going to get tied up in that marriage thing.

JABER   Never in your whole life?

HELENA   Not if I live to be 99. *(levelling camera)* I want you next to the Land Rover. Look happy. Pretend that every one of your wedding parties made your life happier.

JABER   You're thinking about your picture. You're forgetting me. All right. But aren't you like every other woman in the world? Don't you long to be a mother some day?

HELENA   A mother? Sure. Why not? I can be a mother any time I like.

JABER   Without a husband?

HELENA   Without a husband.

JABER   Fatherless children!

HELENA   They wouldn't need a father with a mother like me!

JABER   You'd make an ideal mother. But a child wants a
           father whose name he can carry. Doesn't he?

HELENA   He could choose any name he liked. Look I want a
           real smile. That's a little better. *(Takes picture)* Still, I
           don't want to have kids. I've got Agamemnon.

JABER   Who's Agamemnon?

HELENA   Don't you mock him. He's the most beautiful cat in
           the world. And the brightest. He's a Siamese, if that
           means anything to you, pure Siamese with a pedigree
           to make Prince Charles look like a test-tube baby. My
           flatmate's looking after him ... He's everything to me.

JABER   Just this one cat?

HELENA   You'll understand. Look. *(She produces a small
           album from her handbag)* It's a photo album. Filled
           with pictures of Agamemnon. But there's one page
           empty, just room for a picture of the gazelle you're
           going to catch for me.

JABER   Won't there be room for a picture of Jaber?

           (HELENA shows him pictures in the album)

HELENA   Here he is sleeping in his Waitrose box. He has a
           proper basket but he won't use it. At about four in the
           morning he climbs out of that old cardboard box and
           marches up and down on me before he settles to sleep
           on my shoulder. Imagine! In my flat I'll have a cat and
           a gazelle, the cat sleeping on my shoulder, the gazelle
           on my feet. I'll take them both to the park with me on
           crimson leads. We'll browse in my local second-hand
           bookshop, they have lots of cat books but not much on

20

gazelles so we'll complain. Then a quick one at the Mog and Antelope – one lager, one bowl of milk and a plate of sandy water. On the way home we'll drop in to the supermarket to pick up our supper – a frozen pizza, a tin of Kit-e-Kat and a packet of Gazello Crunchies. People sometimes object to dogs. But I've never heard any moans about cats and gazelles. People will go all googley-eyed. The gossip columnists will write about us: 'A girl with a cat is one thing. A girl who shares her bed with a cat and a gazelle is something else. The mind boggles. And so, I'd wager, does the bed.' But what'll we call my gazelle. Electra? Antigone? Andromeda? I'm in love with Greek legends.

JABER   Not just one gazelle. I will hunt three or four for you. I'll send you home with all your wishes granted ... I mean it.

HELENA   Thank you very much. Here he is eating his tea. I give it to him first thing when I come home from work. I've never left him to go on a trip before. Wonder how he's managing without me to take care of him?

JABER   I wish you'd take care of me, too.

HELENA   How d'you mean, Jaber?

JABER   All your love goes to Mr. Victor. I have to stay all shivering alone. There are three of us. Enlarge the circle of your love, so that it includes me.

HELENA   Who said I don't love you? And here he is at the local cat show. He won third prize. There's the medal round his neck.

JABER   I'm beginning to love this cat. I want you to love me as a woman loves a man. You are beautiful, the desert is empty. Love me for a little while.

(He tries to embrace her but she pushes him away)

21

HELENA   If Victor heard you he'd go crazy. Don't you want to see the rest of my pictures?

JABER   Do you love him?

HELENA   Agamemnon?

JABER   No, Victor.

HELENA   I don't believe in instant love. And there's the gap between our ages. But I do owe him something. I had a dream about the desert. He made it come true. And here he is when I gave him a birthday party. Can't you see how happy he is, laughing with his whiskers? It was an unpretentious little party. Just Agamemnon and me and my friend Joanna and her cat Mutton.

JABER   So between you and Victor, it's not love. It's a mutual interest in the desert. What an astonishing people you are! With your cat's birthdays.

HELENA   If you feel lonely, why didn't you bring your wife along? We wouldn't have minded.

JABER   This is your excursion, Madam. We do not make picnics in the desert. I only came because I had to. This desert has eaten up my life.

HELENA   *(looking at photo of cat)* Oh I do wish I could've brought him with me.

JABER   It's different for visitors. For them the desert's a novelty. But I've been travelling with the caravans ever since I was small. Crossing and re-crossing the desert on camel back. The journey could take months. In the old days the desert was a terrible monster. Sandstorms would suddenly rise up and swallow down an entire caravan. I've seen the sun pour down out of the sky like a stream of molten steel. So hot a man could die on his feet. Winds howled around us and covered over the tracks we were following. Or the water ran out and we had to drink the liquid from the

22

camels' stomachs till we were rescued. For me this is an empty space, not a holiday resort.

HELENA   You're making me frightened of the desert.

JABER   Good.

          (VICTOR re-enters cheerfully. Puts toilet roll in Land Rover)

VICTOR   Had a hunch. Could be a thing with the starter motor. *(Fiddles with engine)* Ah yes.

JABER   But the desert has changed. Of course it has. Aeroplanes. Helicopters. They conquer thirst and wind and sand and heat and cold. They trim the claws of this wild desert. Now there are asphalt roads linking the towns. Bedouins are living in houses, in streets of houses. And new inhabitants have arrived. The oil companies – with their drills like great black trees in the sands. And their pipelines stretching like veins across the desert. But still the desert is too big for them. The desert is greater than all of us. There remain areas which no man would dare to cross.

HELENA   But aren't you frightened by the desert's emptiness? Oh, and this one. Look, he's having his bath. Aren't you terrified when you're alone?

JABER   Your cat lives like a prince. No, the desert doesn't frighten me. But it always makes me feel small and insignificant. Fear? I've always lived with fear ever since they put a dagger in my hand and said: 'Don't leave the house without this. The sons of the tribe of Othman want to take their revenge by killing you.' I was only 11 at the time. 'They want to kill me?' 'Yes. This is your dagger. Be a man. Defend yourself with it.' Can you imagine? A child a little over ten years old. Fear was a stone that they placed in my heart. I didn't understand about revenge. I didn't know who the sons of the tribe of Othman were. I've seen people dying. I've fought in battles. I've been wounded. I've

23

faced death many times in the desert. But that was the greatest fear of my life. And even today, I still don't know who the sons of Othman are. There are tribes called Othman scattered all over the desert. But I still carry that dagger. And the stone of fear is still in my heart. Every day when I wake up I ask myself if the sons of the tribe of Othman will strike today. What a cat! Here he is with a book between his feet.

HELENA   Paws.

JABER   He's the first educated cat I ever met. What's his name? Aga ... Aga ...

HELENA   Agamemnon. He was a great hero. He fought for ten years in the Trojan Wars but the day he got home he was murdered by his wife and her feller. But how d'you manage to carry on day to day with these sons of Othman after your throat.

JABER   Don't worry about me. Here he is, heading a ball like Pele. A miraculous cat! *(closes the album)* Look, I have an amulet that wards off all evil. My mother, Allah rest her soul, placed it round my neck in the first week of my life and I've worn it ever since. It's all that keeps me safe.

VICTOR   *(Head in engine)* She's coming along. Any minute now.

          (JABER gives the album back to HELENA, who puts it in her handbag. JABER starts gathering up the pots, pans and plates which are scattered around)

JABER   You've known him long?

HELENA   I don't know him.

JABER   Then why did you come flying out here when he called as if you'd been lovers since the beginning of time?

24

HELENA	Kismet.

JABER	What?

HELENA	Fate. Chance. A West End reception. Champagne cocktails to celebrate the discovery of a new oilfield. Victor was one of the team. I told him I'd dreamed of visiting the desert. He said: 'Come visit us next year'. I forgot all about it till his message hit my desk. So, here I am.

JABER	And your parents agreed straightaway?

HELENA	My parents? What's it got to do with them. Course I love them, but I haven't been to see them for three years. They live ages from London. Yorkshire. No, I tell a lie. I did see my mother last year at Euston and we said hello.

JABER	Hello?

HELENA	Yeh. Hello! Hello Mother. Hello Helena. That was it.

JABER	Didn't Agamemnon teach you about loyalty? And gratitude? Hello? Was that all?

HELENA	Oh no, we stopped for a coffee and chat and I told her I worked for this building society so she asked me to help her get a loan to buy a new house.

JABER	But you were feeling ungrateful so you refused?

HELENA	Course not. I fixed the loan for her that afternoon. It was a gift.

JABER	So now you understand the pleasure of giving to one's parents.

HELENA	I don't mean a gift to her.

JABER	A gift to your conscience then?

HELENA   No, the one per cent.

JABER   One per cent what?

HELENA   Commission.

JABER   Commission for you?

HELENA   Naturally.

JABER   One per cent from your mother?

HELENA   What's wrong with that? I get one per cent of the value of the house. My mother gets the loan. Everybody's happy.

JABER   That sort of thing freezes my heart. The desert I grew up in doesn't terrify me. But I am truly terrified by this other desert.

          (VICTOR climbs into the Land Rover, shaking his head. It starts first time. He smiles)

VICTOR   OK everyone let's get a move on folding up these beds and the tent. We need to press on before it's too hot. This is meant to be a hunting trip.

          (Meanwhile HELENA has taken off her clothes to reveal a bikini. She goes and splashes water over her body. Then dries her body, brings out a suntan lotion, sits in a chair and begins to apply the lotion)

HELENA   Hang about, Victor, I haven't sunbathed yet. I'm crazy about the sun. He's like a great big golden lover. When the sun pours down on me I feel like a Steinway being played by Oscar Peterson. And it's all thanks to you, Victor. You're a love.

VICTOR   I'm more of a Richard Clayderman fan myself. Let's have a little taste. One for the road if there was a road. Let's have a Scotch, Jaber.

(JABER brings the bottle with a glass)

JABER   Isn't it a little early in the day for whisky?

VICTOR   And a glass for Helena. *(JABER brings another glass)* What about you, Jaber?

JABER   You know I don't drink, Mr. Victor. You'll excuse me now? I must go to pray. Perhaps Allah will bless our journey.

(JABER goes to the edge of the stage and begins his ritual ablutions, using sand instead of water)

HELENA   *(laughing)* What's he up to now? What's this sand business, Jaber?

JABER   When we have no water we use the pure sands of the deserts to wash in before we make our prayers.

HELENA   But there's plenty of water.

JABER   There is never plenty of water. This is the desert and every drop of water is precious. Never forget that. Allah Akbar.

(He begins his prayers)

VICTOR   And every drop of Scotch is precious too. *(He fills the two glasses and begins to hum Take a Pair of Sparking Eyes)*

HELENA   I think he's ticking us off for washing ourselves with water.

VICTOR   Let's drink a toast. The desert!

(VICTOR clinks glasses with her, kisses her quickly and continues humming)

HELENA   He really is a bit weird.

27

VICTOR   Leave him to me.

                (To JABER) – All right, where's the gazelles? That's
                what we came to the desert for – gazelles, not God.
                Are you deaf?

                *(VICTOR finishes his glass and fills another while
                JABER continues to pray. VICTOR and HELENA
                exchange kisses and laugh)*

HELENA   He asked me why you don't get married.

VICTOR   What did you tell him?

HELENA   I said you had dedicated your life to science.

VICTOR   I must have better reasons than that. No, I've never
                found a place where I wanted to settle down. And I'm
                not keen on a permanent woman around the place
                permanently asking me those permanent questions:
                where? How? Who? When? Why? But Helena, most
                important reason: If I'd been married we wouldn't be
                here together in the clean, wild air of the desert. I'm
                beginning to feel young and alive again, I can feel it
                happening.

HELENA   Great. I've got some friends at work. We were
                planning a sea cruise holiday together. And saving up.
                But I passed up the ocean for the desert.

                *(JABER has finished his prayers and is now holding a
                set of beads)*

JABER   As the servant who stands at the gateway of the Palace
                of the Desert I say to you: 'Welcome!' The desert is
                flattered to be chosen when you might have favoured
                the ocean.

HELENA   Maybe Neptune's angry with me now.

JABER   Neptune?

HELENA   God of the sea.

JABER   If the sea-god is angry, he can go drink the sea water.
           It should be enough for you, Helena, that the desert
           loves you.

HELENA   *(jumping up as if suddenly hit)* Let's go, let's go. The
           sun's eating me up. I'm ready.

           *(She puts on her clothes. VICTOR offers her another
           glass of whisky and they begin to get ready to leave,
           packing up things in the car)*

VICTOR   Due south, is it?

JABER   Yes. Take a dead straight line. Before noon tomorrow
           we'll have reached the final stage.

           *(HELENA is busy taking photos of them as they pack
           up)*

VICTOR   Sure we've got everything? Water, food, petrol,
           medicine chest? Mustn't take risks in the desert.

JABER   Everything OK.

VICTOR   And the whisky. That's my responsibility.

JABER   And the Land Rover.

VICTOR   My responsibility.

JABER   It is. Most valuable item on our journey. More
           precious even than food or water.

VICTOR   I've got enough spare parts to make two more Land
           Rovers.

           *(VICTOR jumps into the driver's seat humming the
           Dam Busters' March. JABER and HELENA join in the
           singing but delay getting into the car so as to make
           sure that they've forgotten nothing. VICTOR turns on*

the engine)

JABER   That exhaust. You're spoiling the good air with your
blue smoke.

VICTOR   Get a move on or I'll leave you to the desert.

JABER   I couldn't ask for a more glorious fate. Leave us two
here.

*(JABER comes to HELENA while they are still
singing. He takes her in his arms. She resists at first.
They are behind the Land Rover, where VICTOR can't
see them. Soon HELENA submits to JABER and they
fall into a long embrace. VICTOR sounds his horn.
HELENA slips out of JABER's arms and jumps in to
the back seat of the Land Rover while JABER stays
rooted to the spot as if he can't believe what has
happened until he sees the car begin to move. He
jumps into the front passenger seat while they all
carry on singing)*

VICTOR   This is your Captain speaking. I would like to
welcome you aboard and wish you all a pleasant
flight.

(The wind begins to rise. They are driving along now)

VICTOR   I thought we were supposed to run into your gazelles a
few miles after the village.

JABER   They're shyer these days. After they first discovered
human beings, the gazelles fled to the ends of the
earth. Once they used to love this region, they'd even
wander down our village street. No matter how many
of them we hunted down, there were always more
gazelles. But then visitors came to the Kingdom and
they hunted the gazelles for sport. And oil companies
came to the Kingdom and began to examine the
desert, inch by inch, like doctors examining the body
of a patient. And the gazelles began to fade away, to
die away. Very few of them reached the depths of the

desert, beyond the reach of the oil companies. There was a law to forbid the hunting of gazelles, but they went on dying and the law was forgotten.

VICTOR   But you said we'd have good hunting round here.

(They are still driving across the desert)

JABER   Don't worry, you'll meet the gazelles. I shall introduce you. Gazelles, this is Mr. Victor. He is a good and gracious gentleman and wishes you no harm. But he would like to take a few of you and present you as a gift to his lady friend Helena. You will be luxuriously and kindly cared for. That's what I'll tell them, and the rest's up to you. OK?

VICTOR   *(laughs)* OK. Fine.

JABER   Nobody knows the gazelles like me. As a boy I used to ride my camel through the desert searching for food for my family. And then I began my little war against the gazelles. I would stay six or seven days and nights lying in wait for them. And I'd travel back with a camel laden with the bodies of gazelles. So I could feed my family and sell the rest of the meat in the village. When one of my sons died I thought it was a punishment for killing those gazelles. But I didn't have any other trade. All I knew was the desert. So I had to become a guide for companies and tourists. If there was any other job in the world, I'd quit. I've been promised a chance of being a night-watchman in a garage. Guarding the shining cars in a cool concrete cave. I'd happily leave this job because I know the gazelles hate me. Some day they'll destroy me if I don't leave them alone. If they had newspapers you'd read about me every day – Jaber – public enemy number one of the Gazelles. It worries me, it scares me.

VICTOR   You're exaggerating, Jaber. If you can fix those gazelles for us, I promise you a job as a messenger at the company's offices in town. *(Looks at notebook)*

31

We get back on the Sunday. Then there's a holiday ... then a weeks' holiday. Third week ... Monday morning the section heads meet. Evening there's laboratory committee. Tuesday's full up. Wednesday I'll take care of your job ... Wednesday, 10 am, three weeks from now. Turn up on the dot and it's fixed. *(He writes down the appointment)*

JABER   That's very good of you, but just a moment. *(He consults an invisible diary)* Three weeks' time ... morning, a meeting with the Directors. Afternoon – consultations with clients. Evening – an appointment with a strange woman – what? My secretary didn't say anything about this ... It's to dine with you, Madame Helena. *(She wakes from a short nap and is surprised as she doesn't know what's going on)* That's what my diary says. You'd better stop sunbathing in the desert or we'll spend a month treating all the burns on your soft body. I'll have a word with my secretary and cancel all your appointments. *(Seriously)* But I've come to hate this job. I don't want any more gazelles. I'll be happy working in the company. There'll be new kinds of gazelles – blonde gazelles from Canada, America, Rome, Paris and London. Merciful Allah! What a golden opportunity.

VICTOR   You needn't feel so bad. We want to take these gazelles alive.

JABER   Mr. Victor, have you ever seen a gazelle die?

VICTOR   'Course not. Been much too busy.

JABER   My shot hit the creature. I ran up, all happy. I'd got the gazelle I wanted. It wasn't dead yet. It was jerking its body. The agony was beating in it. And slowly it twisted up its face towards me, and its teeth were bared in pain. And it looked at me. And its eyes were filled with contempt. I'll never forget. The most beautiful black eyes. Black eyes staring up into my eyes. And I saw a tear shining.

VICTOR	Come on –
JABER	Yes. It was weeping. Gazelles do weep. And it stared at me like a traitor, as if I'd broken some sort of promise. As if there had been some kind of pledge between us and I had broken it. The gazelle kept looking at me until it died. I was full of wonder. I put out my hand and closed its eyes - that dying saint. When I stood up I was shivering like a man stricken with sudden fever. I left the gazelle where it lay and walked back to my village. And there I found that my sick son had died.
HELENA	I'm sorry.
JABER	*(to VICTOR)* Slower. Slow down.
VICTOR	What's the matter?
HELENA	*(looking through field glasses)* There they are.
VICTOR	What? *(He sees)* Unbelievable.
HELENA	So many ... so many ...
VICTOR	Crowding together. Like pilgrims at Mecca.
JABER	Slowly ...
HELENA	Like they've come from all over the world.
VICTOR	So many ...
JABER	Slowly, close in slowly.
HELENA	And I was hoping to see just one.
VICTOR	And suddenly the whole world's filled with them. All ages, all colours ...
HELENA	There must be some reason. One of their Princes is getting married. The coronation of their King. The

33

Kingdom of gazelles.

VICTOR   Gazelles! Gazelles! *(He keeps shouting and the others join in)*

ALL   Gazelles! Gazelles! Gazelles!

(The stage is filled with gazelles. VICTOR, HELENA, and JABER gaze around them, silently, for a long time, as gazelles surround them)

END OF ACT ONE

ACT TWO

(The desert. Sunset. The Land Rover, surrounded by gazelles. VICTOR, JABER, and HELENA in the Land Rover, staring at them)

HELENA   *(quietly)* Gazelles. Gazelles.

(HELENA moves as if to climb out of the Land Rover. JABER holds her back)

JABER   *(whispering)* I never saw so many. Even before the oil came. So many of them.

HELENA   Let me out, Jaber. I'll catch one. *(She moves suddenly)*

VICTOR   No!

(The gazelles wheel and start to run. VICTOR starts to drive after them. They begin to outrun him. But a stray gazelle is cut off from the rest of the group and pauses, uncertain where to run. VICTOR stops the Land Rover and stares at the creature)

VICTOR   My God. The most beautiful creature ... Look how her body's shaped for speed, so she can glide over the desert like a little yacht. And her colour! Golden-brown circles on snow. All this in the sunset. Looks like she's made out of fire. She's a glowing sapphire.

JABER   A sapphire in the hand of an invisible giant.

(The gazelle takes flight. VICTOR gives chase)

HELENA   Looks like the giant's making a dash for it.

VICTOR   Got to chase it. It's all I can do.

HELENA   If only we can catch it, and take it home with us. I've never seen anything as beautiful.

35

(The ride becomes bumpier. The sun sets gradually during this part to be replaced by the rising moon)

VICTOR   We'll get it.

JABER   I don't know.

VICTOR   Any minute. It's bound to collapse. Look, there it goes.

(The gazelle staggers and seems to fall in front of the Land Rover. VICTOR stops the car, but the gazelle rises and runs off again. VICTOR starts up the car. He drives in a frenzy. The wind howls)

VICTOR   Damn it.

JABER   You've got a rifle. It's loaded.

(They are all shouting to make themselves heard)

VICTOR   I don't want to kill it.

HELENA   Don't kill it.

VICTOR   I want to hunt it down. I want to take it alive. Want to keep it.

JABER   But you lost all the others – those uncountable gazelles. All for the sake of one. Slow down.

VICTOR   They don't matter. This is the one.

JABER   Slow down. Better turn back. We're getting into the black zone.

HELENA   What' that?

VICTOR   Don't try and stop me.

JABER   Stop! It's dangerous. It's an area of death.

HELENA	Listen to him. Stop.
JABER	*(pulling at VICTOR's shirt)* Stop. Slow down.
VICTOR	I've got to have it. I can't stop. It'll collapse again soon. Then I'll have it. A present for Helena. Gazelle! I'm coming for you.
JABER	Stop.
HELENA	Victor, please stop now.
JABER	He's like cement and steel.
HELENA	He can't hear us.
JABER	Possessed by devils.
HELENA	Fighting for his life.
JABER	Slow down. Help.

(The Land Rover is crashing and bouncing. VICTOR hits his head, which begins to bleed)

VICTOR	God – I'm coming after you.
JABER	You're hurt. Let me take over.

(JABER and VICTOR struggle for the steering wheel. VICTOR fights off JABER)

HELENA	*(to JABER)* We ought to jump out.
JABER	We'd be killed.
HELENA	He's crazy.
JABER	Better pray. *(He begins to recite the Koran)*
HELENA	I can't pray. I'll sing.

(HELENA bawls out a rock song – something on the lines of Little Richard's Good Golly Miss Molly – trying to sing so hard she'll survive)

(By now it is moonlight on a black landscape)

JABER   We're right in the heart of it. The black zone.

HELENA   Stop, Victor. You're bleeding.

VICTOR   Let me catch it first. Let me – where is it?

(VICTOR stops the Land Rover)

HELENA   Vanished.

JABER   Like a ghost.

VICTOR   Nothing?

HELENA   The blood. Let me bandage you.

VICTOR   I don't give a damn about the blood! I want my gazelle.

JABER   It's gone.

VICTOR   Nothing.

HELENA   Black mountains. Moonlight. And the howling of a wind that fills the world.

(The wind rises to a climax)

VICTOR   Where are we?

(It is as if VICTOR is waking from a dream. He is in shock. HELENA starts to bandage his head)

JABER   We're lost, I think.

38

HELENA   In the black zone.

VICTOR   *(screaming at JABER)* Get me out of this bloody mess!

HELENA   He didn't get you into it. What are we going to do?

VICTOR   Nice quiet drive home. *(Tries to start the Land Rover. Fails. Tries again. Fails)* Shit. Folks, we seem to have run out of petrol.

HELENA   That's not funny.

VICTOR   No it's not. Pass the Johnny Walker. And then let's get some sodding sleep.

> *(VICTOR, JABER and HELENA freeze as HELENA passes the bottle. Fade to black. Lights up and the time is now shortly after sunrise days later. VICTOR is huddled in the driving seat, fast asleep. JABER is in the passenger seat, looking washed-out. HELENA is trying to sleep in the back seat. All three are covered from head to toe in dust)*

JABER   You asleep?

HELENA   Asleep? I'm being beaten on the head with a white-hot hammer. Bang, bang, bang, bang. Like a bloody disco.

> *(JABER climbs out of the Land Rover. He picks up a handful of dust. Looks at it)*

What's that? Breakfast?

JABER   Trying to work out where we are. By the nature of the dust, you know. Pass the binoculars, please. *(She does)* Should be an oil company prospecting. Somewhere round here.

> *(JABER moves away from the Land Rover, scanning the area through the binoculars. VICTOR wakes up, raises his head, looks around as if trying to identify*

the place. His clothes are spattered with blood and his head is bandaged. He wipes the dust from his face)

VICTOR   Where the hell? What happened? I'm still in a nightmare. Am I?

HELENA   Have a look in the petrol can. Maybe there's a few drops left. A few drops? Enough to get us away from this damn black earth.

VICTOR   I knew it'd happen. Oh, my back, ow. Pain in my neck too. And my legs. When we started out, I had this premonition. My blood suddenly stopped.

HELENA   You could have told us. I really appreciate it when friends tell me their premonitions of doom except that ninety-nine times out of a hundred premonitions of doom don't come true. But I'll make an exception in your case.

VICTOR   How long have I been behind this bloody useless wheel?

HELENA   My muscles won't work. I was scared by that storm. Like a million wolves were howling. Not in harmony either.

VICTOR   The wolves didn't eat us. But this is worse than wolves. Maybe that bedouin of ours wanted this to happen. Had it in for us all along. Set a trap for us. Humiliate us, insult us – and then get rid of us. I know these desert bedouin. They've hated us all through history.

HELENA   He's not so bad. We're all in the same ... boat. And Jaber's climbed up the mast in the hope of spotting dry land.

VICTOR   I don't trust people who eat snakes.

(They climb down heavily from the Land Rover, wiping dust and dirt from their faces and clothes)

HELENA   What do we do now?

(VICTOR strides to the rear of the Land Rover looking for petrol in the empty cans. He throws them out, one after another. No petrol. HELENA collapses and sits on one of the cans. VICTOR loses all hope and turns on JABER)

VICTOR   Any sign of land?

JABER   Nothing moving. My friends, we are face to face with a rather ugly problem.

VICTOR   It's your fault. Four days we've been lost. Four days wandering around. Four days covered in dust. Four days of the wind howling. Four days going round in circles, guided by a bloody blind man. Thanks.

JABER   There is a sort of track. We're lucky to find that.

VICTOR   I'm very glad to have the opinion of the world's leading authority on the desert. The man who claims to know the Sahara like the back of his hand. What's the use of a track with no bloody petrol?

JABER   You're the one who took us into the black zone.

VICTOR   No. The gazelle did. I'm hungry!

JABER   I'll get the food ready. *(From the Land Rover he pulls out a box. It is full of sand. He looks for and finds a tin of sardines)* Sardines. Bread. *(Opens a nylon bag and takes out bread. He starts to make sandwiches)*

HELENA   Why can you never starve in the desert?

JABER   You can starve.

HELENA   It's a riddle. Like you have at Christmas. A silly riddle.

JABER	Why can you never starve in the desert?
HELENA	Because of the sand which is there!
VICTOR	Jesus.
JABER	I don't understand. But there's sand in everything.
HELENA	What's the black zone?
JABER	People don't get out of it. Caravans of hundreds of people have come here and disappeared. Even the oil companies, with all their machinery, they steer clear of the zone. There was one oil expedition. It was a disaster. Luckily help came quickly. They had to leave all their gear behind. The crew just got out in helicopters. This is the great Sahara. And now you know a little about it.
VICTOR	I know a bit about the Sahara. But I know more about under the ground than what's on the surface. You're an expert on its skin. I specialise in the bowels. You're my guide to the surface.
HELENA	I can't eat this. It's full of sand.
VICTOR	I can't eat it.
JABER	But it's the most delicious food in the world. You'll find that out in a few hours time. I'm just amazed that we're still alive. I don't know why the Land Rover didn't sink into the sand. There were thousands of rocks sticking out of the ground like black daggers. Why didn't the tyres get torn to shreds? This place is full of evil spirits. You ought to be grateful that we're still alive. It's a miracle.
HELENA	Funny. I want civilisation very badly.
VICTOR	The gazelle. The gazelle – for you. That's all I could think about. That's why I drove like that.

JABER	You nearly killed us.
VICTOR	The gazelle.
JABER	The gazelle's fault, of course. It drove you mad.
HELENA	We shouldn't have gone round and round and round and round, on and on and on. We should have stopped for a while to think.
JABER	We had to keep moving. Otherwise we'd have been buried in sand.
HELENA	I'm just beginning to feel the pain. Like my body's been beaten with salty whips. My head's like a gyroscope. What do we do now? What'll you do, Jaber?
VICTOR	He's done enough.
HELENA	That's not fair. What could he do? How could he stop you driving like an over-age Jimmy Dean?
VICTOR	It was for you. It was all for you. And now you turn on me –
JABER	Shall we calm down? There's a problem, that's for sure. But others have faced the same problem.
VICTOR	Any survivors?
JABER	A few.
VICTOR	Great. That's great!
JABER	In a case like this.
VICTOR	What in a case like this?
JABER	The first golden rule is to keep our heads.
VICTOR	Now I know where I met you before.

JABER   Where?

VICTOR The Hitchhiker's Guide to the Galaxy. 'Don't Panic.'
        You know? No, of course you don't.

JABER   That's right – don't panic.

VICTOR Don't panic. OK.

JABER   Sure there's no petrol?

VICTOR Sure.

JABER   But we've got food and drink.

VICTOR For how long?

JABER   Three days? It depends. On top of that we've found a
        track. Somebody must use it, sometime. So why
        panic?

VICTOR Good question. What's the second golden rule?

JABER   Stay by the car. It's easy to see from the air.

VICTOR For the buzzards?

JABER   For the search party.

VICTOR If there's a search party.

JABER   Yes. And the car is our big protector against the sun.

VICTOR So we just sit about and stare into space?

JABER   Don't make fun of staring into space. Revelation from
        Allah only fell upon those who sat and contemplated
        in the desert.

VICTOR I didn't realise you had such aspirations.

JABER	But we'll do more than sit and contemplate. We'll collect firewood. We'll keep a fire going all night. That'll guide our rescuers.
VICTOR	Scorpions and snakes. Great God Almighty!
JABER	May your heart be filled with faith.
VICTOR	Sometimes I think you're winding me up.
JABER	How?
VICTOR	Making fun of me.
JABER	God forbid! How could someone like me around someone like you? You have fame and money and New York and London and hotels like glass mountains and helicopters whizzing through the air as obediently as hunting dogs – and me – I'm a miserable bedouin and I have nothing at all.
VICTOR	You get it all mixed up, don't you? Serious talk and joking. With you I don't know where one begins and the other ends. This isn't a good time for jokes, Jaber. We sit here, and death is sitting beside us.
JABER	The justice of the desert is very cruel.
HELENA	My head's cracking open.
VICTOR	I'm stiff all over. Feel like I'm made of wood. My arms and legs don't seem part of me any more. All right, Jaber, you can laugh. You haven't been driving this bugger. Stupid bloody Land Rover.
HELENA	Give me something for my head.

(JABER goes to medicine chest for aspirin. He comes back to her with a glass of water)

JABER	Swallow this pill. You'll feel better. Don't worry, it'll be all right. As soon as we've found some petrol we'll

45

go after those gazelles again and this time we'll catch you one.

HELENA   All I want is to get shot of this headache. The gazelle's gone. I couldn't give a shit about it.

(All three lean against the petrol cans near the Land Rover. JABER throws to the other two blankets and pillows. By the car he sets up a kind of sunshade to protect them from the heat of the sun. He offers a drink to each of them)

HELENA   I want my radio. What' going on in the world? Is there a world? I think we're all alone.

(She goes to the Land Rover to look for the radio)

JABER   Oh no. The desert's full of wandering spirits. Sometimes they're in the form of women, sometimes in the form of a whole caravan. You see it in the distance – men, women, tents and camels. They're all enjoying a party, dancing and singing, and you run to join in the fun and you're smiling at them and suddenly – shiff! – no party, no dancing, no singing. Not even the shadow of a camel. You see, it was a wedding party of spirits. And sometimes the spirits take the form of gazelles. I'm thinking about that. That gazelle, all alone, that damn beautiful gazelle who led us into the black zone – maybe it was nothing but a female spirit who wanted to enchant us. And she took us to the zone, and she left us there. And now she's laughing her head off. Some spirits are famous for their sense of humour.

HELENA   The radio's full of sand. The whole world's been silted up. All the world's music is buried under the sand dunes. And the bloody quiz programmes too. *(Tries the camera)* And my camera's jammed. It's weird. First the Land Rover goes on strike and now the radio and the camera come out in sympathy. Civilisation has skidded to a halt. It's back to basics. It's like the day before the Creation – a great silent void with no trace of Elvis Costello. I'm beginning to believe in your spirits.

VICTOR Desert people have an explanation for everything. Anything strange gets blamed on the spirits.

HELENA I think there was a trap. A trap set for us. That gazelle was sent to seduce us with its beauty and lead us here. And we get here. And what happens? The fuel tank dries up. The radio and the camera and the taper get filled with dust and kick the electronic bucket. And now it's our turn. It's a plot. By somebody, something. It must be. *(She stands up)* Come on. Let's get away.

VICTOR *(taking hold of her)* Sit down. Helena. Sit down. Let's just talk quietly.

HELENA Why?

VICTOR To pass the time till we can get some sleep. All we can do is wait.

HELENA Wait to be dead?

VICTOR Wait to be rescued.

JABER Maybe you can jiggle round the wires of this radio? Maybe it would turn into a transmitter.

VICTOR I'm an oil engineer, not a radio engineer.

JABER I apologise. You're an oil engineer. Well, that's good. We've got a Land Rover here, empty. But look at the energy all round.

VICTOR What?

JABER You've got the sun and the desert. And all that lies underneath the desert.

VICTOR I know how to be an oil engineer. Shame you don't know how to be a guide.

HELENA   *(Tries vainly to make the radio work – then flings it away)* Let's go! Who would rescue us here? Will an angel flap down and carry us home to Heathrow?

JABER   I don't think I'll be reported missing for ages. And I don't suppose you will be either, Helena. But Allah be praised, we've got a famous man with us. If he's a day or two late returning, his company will send the whole Army to search for him. So let's not worry.

VICTOR   But I didn't tell the company about this trip.

HELENA   Why not?

VICTOR   Because you're listed on my pass documents as a male guide. And I didn't want my colleagues sticking their noses in my business.

JABER   And he also thought it best not to tell our village policeman – in case the Morals Squad took an interest. I don't know what you were so scared about. They wouldn't come and arrest her just for going on a hunting trip.

VICTOR   I didn't tell anyone except the garage where I hired the Land Rover. I asked for a transmitter. But they're only allowed to fit them for the army and police.

HELENA   Is the garage man a friend?

VICTOR   Hardly knows me.

JABER   At least he'll miss his Land Rover. But not for a while. It's worse than I thought.

HELENA   I don't understand – you trying to keep this trip secret. And you're saying it's because of me. Like I was shameful, like I was something dirty you want to hide away. We're supposed to be hunting gazelles in this desert, not satisfying some passing desire of yours.

JABER	Every man must struggle to satisfy his lasting desires.
VICTOR	You stay out of this one!
JABER	The quarry has been lost – but the desire has been achieved.
VICTOR	I said – stay out of this. *(To HELENA)* That's what you think of me? I'm sorry I asked you!
HELENA	I'm sorry I came!
VICTOR	This whole trip was for you.
JABER	How can we pass the time? I do know a game where two men compete in manhood.
VICTOR	Oh?
JABER	But for that we would need another woman. *(He laughs)*
VICTOR	What a nasty-minded bedouin!
JABER	Does it offend you to talk about sex? I think it's the best thing in the world. I hope Allah hasn't taken it away from you.
VICTOR	You shut up or I'll bust your skull.
JABER	It's the truth that makes you angry.
VICTOR	*(jumping to his feet and approaching JABER threateningly)* You filthy little bastard.
HELENA	I can't stay. The air's poisoned.
	(Exit HELENA)
VICTOR	Helena, don't be absurd! *(to JABER).* You see?
JABER	Can't take a joke?

VICTOR   No – your humour's above my head. Helena! Helena!

JABER   Don't kill yourself running after her. Where can she go?

VICTOR   She's not stopping. She may just carry on till she collapses.

JABER   Or maybe she'll run across a bedouin caravan or an oil rig. And we'll all be saved.

VICTOR   Is that another one of your desert jokes? Go and apologise to her. Go on. Then she'll come back.

JABER   She won't go far.

HELENA   *(Offstage)* Help! Jaber! Victor! Help!

JABER   See?

(Both run off to rescue her but she runs on before they go off stage. VICTOR takes her in his arms and helps her to sit down. She is still suffering from shock. JABER goes off to investigate)

VICTOR   You all right? Helena? What happened?

(HELENA points off stage, still in panic)

HELENA   There! Over there!

VICTOR   Was it a wolf?

(JABER enters carrying a skull)

JABER   Was that it, Helena? a few bones and skulls? I thought you were tougher than that. It's just like I told Victor – I said you'd come across a bedouin caravan. Or maybe it's some soldiers left over from the war. The Germans, the Italians and the Allies had a battle round here. Maybe it's the skull of a British officer. Do you

50

	recognise him? A very respectable-looking skull. Salute him. It's General Death.
VICTOR	Pack it in, clown. There's another bottle of Scotch. Go fetch it.

(JABER fetches the bottle of whisky and a glass full of sand. VICTOR wipes the sand away and hands a drink to HELENA. He drinks straight from the bottle)

VICTOR	Take this, it'll settle your nerves.
HELENA	Thanks.
JABER	*(to skull)* It was a big mistake, General, to bring your European tribal war to our desert. An intrusion ...
VICTOR	I suppose you want your revenge.
JABER	Not me. I was a boy. But the desert has a memory.
HELENA	I tripped. I fell down. I fell in a dip full of human skulls and human bones. Clustering together. Take that thing away.
JABER	*(to skull)* All right, sir, shall we go?

(JABER goes off stage to put the skull back where it was)

HELENA	Get me out of this wilderness. Get me back to civilisation.
VICTOR	Have another. It won't be long.
HELENA	It's ridiculous. All my friends in the office think I'm having one hell of a gassy time. They're all suffocating in the office and they imagine me riding pillion on a Sheikh's white charger, zooming around the Sahara shooting gazelles.
VICTOR	It'll be all right. We'll laugh about this one day.

51

JABER   Can I have three pieces of paper?

VICTOR   What for?

JABER   I want to write down what each of us eats and drinks.
            So nobody takes more than the others. And maybe one
            day scientists can study my lists and learn something
            about survival diets.

VICTOR   You are an astonishing nutcase. One eye on social
            justice and the other on scientific knowledge. You'll
            find my notebook in the glove compartment.

HELENA   He thinks it's wartime. It'll be clothing coupons next.
            Scotch with no ice tastes ludicrous. Like dandelion
            and burdock.

JABER   (looking in the Land Rover for notebook) This is
            worse than wartime. There's a shortage of people and
            plants and water. You'd never believe this was once a
            forest. There were rivers crowded with fish and water-
            birds, there were cities and palaces and a great
            civilisation.

HELENA   When was that?

JABER   Oh, that was tens of thousands of years ago. Before
            England, I think. And before that, this whole area was
            a great prairie of wild beasts grazing peaceably. But
            now the prairie grass and the forest trees have become
            black oil in the belly of the earth. We dredge up the oil
            and it becomes the blood of our machines.
            Unfortunately our machine has no blood left.

VICTOR   So now you blame the whole thing on the machine?

JABER   I think I knew when it started to go wrong. The day I
            killed my camel.

HELENA   Why did you do that?

52

JABER	To make a feast for the convoy of vehicles searching for oil.
	(There is the sound of an approaching light airplane, tiny at first, then growing)
HELENA	What's that?
VICTOR	What?
JABER	Listen!
	(Silence. They hear the engine. They all talk at once)
HELENA	My God, it's a plane.
JABER	Where's the rifle?
VICTOR	In the back.
	(JABER climbs over to get the rifle, VICTOR jumps into the Land Rover to get it too, but JABER gets is first. HELENA, in her excitement, climbs up into the Land Rover)
HELENA	A yellow plane.
VICTOR	Wait till she's nearly overhead. Then fire in front of her.
HELENA	Will there be room in it?
VICTOR	Doesn't matter. We're saved!
JABER	I'm ready.
VICTOR	Wait for it. Wait for it. *(Sound of engine nearly overhead)* Wait for it. Now!
	(JABER fires)
HELENA	Ray! that's it! That'll do it!

VICTOR   They'll turn back now.

            (All three cheer and hug each other)

JABER   I burned my face with the gun. I don't care!

HELENA   Come on, plane. Come on.

VICTOR   Come on.

HELENA   It's not turning.

VICTOR   They'll be talking about us now. Deciding what to do.
            Then they'll turn.

HELENA   I don't think they're going to turn.

JABER   They'll turn. They've got to turn.

            *(All three watch. The sound of the plane begins to fade
            into the distance. The three climb down from the Land
            Rover. A silence between them)*

HELENA   The buggers. Look. Get me away from those bones. I
            fell on top of them just now. They crunched. They
            were all squashy under me. *(Proffers her glass)* Fill us
            up. No soda? Get me away from here.

VICTOR   Suppose we take all our supplies and set off towards
            the nearest oasis?

JABER   It's not that easy. We'd be dried up and dead in one
            day. If another plane comes over we've got far more
            chance of being spotted here by the Land Rover. And
            if we don't walk our water'll last four times as long.

VICTOR   How did generation after generation of Jabers survive
            in the desert?

JABER   Me, I never went into the desert except on my camel.
            Sometimes the winds would swirl around and cover

up all the tracks. But when I was lost I'd climb on my camel, let it find its way to the nearest village. When my uncle was 90 years old and stone blind he used to travel the desert alone except for his camel.

VICTOR   We don't need a camel. We need a flaming magic carpet.

JABER   You don't have to believe me. But at least camels don't run out of petrol.

HELENA   I don't want to stay here. *(Gets up as if to leave)*

JABER   No choice. Stay here. Save energy by staying still. Please sit down. *(Hands over the notebook to VICTOR)* You write it down.

VICTOR   *(writing down names on separate sheets)* Helena, Victor, Jaber.

JABER   You be responsible for writing down what is given out to each of us. I'll check how much is left.

(JABER goes to the Land Rover, throws away an empty tin and puts the remaining water in one can)

The most important thing is water. You can always find some kind of food in the desert. But you'll never see water – except in your dreams.

VICTOR   Fine new job I've got – Jaber's secretary.

HELENA   Scratch out my name. I don't want your food and drink. I'm on hunger strike till you find somewhere else. I'll stick to Scotch. *(Takes a gulp from her glass)*

JABER   Nothing else but empty tins. We've got enough for two days. Three and a bit days if we're really careful. *(He turns and sees that they're both drinking Scotch)* It would be better to pour the whisky into the sand.

VICTOR   I'll drink if I want.

55

JABER	I don't care what you do to your brain. That's your business. But it makes you thirsty. So you want more water.
HELENA	No. You shan't have it. It's our Scotch. Ours.
VICTOR	It's a coup. A bedouin dictatorship. *(Laughs)*
JABER	Do what you like. But I won't give up a single drop of my water to either of you. Write this down. Jaber – one can of orange juice. *(Opens the can)*
HELENA	Water is rationed.
VICTOR	First he'll stop us drinking. Then he'll ask us to wash with sand. Soon we'll be a couple of perfect Muslims.
JABER	Why not? The moment death touches me, I know I shall walk into a beautiful life – because I'm a faithful Muslim. There will be green gardens and silver rivers. There will be trees illuminated with ripe fruit. There will be fountains of milk and honey and blessed wine. And there will be women more beautiful than the moon. In that paradise I will never be ill or weary or old. And when I walk in those gardens, where will you be?
VICTOR	In the dust, Jaber.
HELENA	It sounds rather like Bermuda. Do we really have to die to go there?
JABER	Of course. But only if you obey Allah and his Prophet.
VICTOR	I'll manage without your gardens. Just leave me alone with my bottle of Scotch. *(Takes a gulp from his glass and pours one for HELENA)*
JABER	I'm not selling paradise. I'm trying to guard you from thirst. I don't think you have ever been thirsty.

VICTOR	OK, OK. It's our last bottle of booze and I'm stricken to announce that it's nearly finished.
JABER	I'll fetch some firewood before the sun gets too hot.

(Exit JABER)

VICTOR	Want any help?
JABER	*(off)* No thanks!
VICTOR	Good man!
JABER	*(off)* Enjoy your last drink.

(HELENA and VICTOR are suddenly depressed when they hear this remark)

HELENA	Victor. I'm scared. Are we really cut off? No cities? No people? No trees? No shops? No fields? No baked beans factories? No wine bars with Miles Davis tapes? Has the whole world been emptied out like a bottle of Tizer? D'you reckon this bloody desert wind has been tearing round the globe, bashing down the bridges and sinking the ships and knotting up the telegraph wires so nobody can contact anybody? Is the Thames choked up with dirty sand? Is the Atlantic dry? Are we the only ones left alive on a planet without water? No water. Are we going to be like all those skull people over there? Dried up bones being trundled by the wind all over this yellow land? Please tell me that Biggles is on his way and that I'll soon be back in my flat and the office and I'll be able to hug Agamemnon again and drink a Scotch with ice and soda. Tell me. Please.
VICTOR	'Course we'll be rescued. Only sorry I didn't tell Richard. He's the only one I trust in the company. We've worked together a long time.
HELENA	What'll we do when the Scotch is gone? Nearly gone. For God's sake, why didn't you tell Richard? I know the one you mean, he's the one who came with you to

the airport to meet me. He seemed a nice man.

VICTOR   I didn't tell him because in one way he's a bit of a child. As soon as he sees you've got something – a new kind of pen, for instance – he has to have it. When he saw you, he wanted you and he hated me because you were with me.

HELENA   Why should he be jealous? Take it easy with the Scotch. Why couldn't you have told him?

VICTOR   I didn't know this'd happen. I didn't want to take any risks. We had twice as much food and petrol as we needed. We had enough spare parts to stock a garage on the M1. If I'd told him, he'd have wanted to come too. And I couldn't have turned him down.

HELENA   Why not?

VICTOR   Well, we're close. And he's the only one who can be a witness for me.

HELENA   Witness? What about?

VICTOR   I was screwed, badly screwed. A few years back they brought in a real phoney, a crook, and they put him in charge of my section. He got hold of all my research papers, took them back with him to the States and published them under his name. Right, instant fame. They made him a Professor of Petroleum Studies and Research. Adviser to the big corporations. Up for the Nobel Prize. Millionaire. Right? And me? I'm still crawling along like a worm in my underground lab, hoping that now and then he'll mention my name so that I get invited to a conference or two. That's the sort of hand-out he tosses me.

HELENA   Why don't you expose him?

VICTOR   I don't know. I make up my mind to do it. And then I stop. Would he destroy me? He's got the clout. But now I think the hell with that. Soon as I get back I'll break him.

HELENA   What a bugger. If I was you I'd strangle him for a start. But I suppose you need proof.

VICTOR   Richard's word will do it. He knew us both. He's promised to stand by me. First thing I'll do when I get back is hold a Press Conference. Spill the whole story. I should do it soon – Richard's got a dodgy heart.

HELENA   Will TV carry the story?

VICTOR   Sure. It'll be an international scandal. 'OIL WORLD ROCKED BY NOBEL PRIZE FRAUD'.

HELENA   You know, Victor, what I miss most in the desert?

VICTOR   Ice?

HELENA   TV. Specially the commercials, Agamemnon likes them too. He sits on my lap and licks his lips when the Kit-e-Kat one comes on. Then he jumps at the screen and sniffs it. He's a fantastic person! You'll meet him if you visit me in London. And he'll let you know right away if he likes you or not. He's no good at hypocrisy. He'll either jump into your lap or scoot out the door.

VICTOR   Back home, in London. Have you got a man, I mean, someone special?

HELENA   Used to, used to. Two, three years ago. He was a diver for the Navy. He went down deep. Never came up. After that, none of my men lasted more than a month. More than a month and it felt like carrying a rucksack full of car batteries. Last one I had ran off with my flatmate. I didn't mind.

VICTOR   So now you're free.

HELENA   If there's anything on your mind, please keep it there till we get out of this mess. *(She stands up and looks all around)* No sign of the Foreign Legion. Jaber's about the size of a sand-grain.

VICTOR   We're alone. I want to tell you something.

HELENA   What about?

VICTOR   About what happened? Our first night. In the tent.

HELENA   You were just a bit tired and flobby. Why mention it now?

VICTOR   Wasn't just tiredness. It was more than that. I've had that trouble for three years now. First I thought it was just working too hard, exhaustion and that. I tried staying away from the lab. Only spent a few hours a week in the office. No luck. So I took a month off and headed for Paris.

HELENA   Why Paris?

VICTOR   You know – Paris equals sex. Cheerful sex. I hung around the Crazy Horse Saloon like a randy schoolboy only I wasn't randy. I tried the best women money could buy. Nothing. I felt absurd and bleak and despised. When I visited the Louvre the Mona Lisa stuck her tongue out at me.

HELENA   There are doctors –

VICTOR   I couldn't go to a doctor.

HELENA   Why not?

VICTOR   I had this idea that only the desert could cure me. The roughness of the ground. The power of the sandstorms. I was sure that once I got out of the fumes of the city to go hunting in the desert, my body would restore itself. But the only woman in my heart was you. Ever since we met in London. You seemed so fresh. So beautiful. Like a young girl out of an old Greek story. Helena, I'm sorry I didn't tell you all this

60

before. But please trust me.

HELENA   You invited me here for a perfectly straightforward gazelle hunt in the Sahara, right? And all the time you thought of me as your fresh, beautiful, Greek impotence doctor? I ought to kick your bum. But what the hell, love. I'm just sorry I couldn't help you.

VICTOR   When I said I'd catch the most beautiful gazelle for your sake – that was true.

HELENA   And now we're stuck in the desert like Jonah in the whale.

VICTOR   Something strange happened when we ran across those gazelles. That huge space ... gazelles in amazing numbers ... I'd waited for that moment all my life. It ran through me like whisky – this feeling – I had been kept apart from these people all my life, but I loved them very deeply and now I'd come home. My own people. And when that lone gazelle appeared and turned to me, I felt a sudden change in my bones, all through my body. My strength was coming back. My blood had been stagnant for three years and now it was boiling up through my veins again. Something exploded. I was young again. New again. And I was off after that gazelle. There was nothing else in the world. Every cell in my body was fully alive. I've never known anything like it before.

          (A moment of silence)

HELENA   I understand now.

          (Silence)

VICTOR   And then it was a dream – a gone dream.

          (HELENA tries to say something, stops. She comes near him and puts her hand on his)

HELENA   Victor. *(Silence)* Shall I tell you something? *(VICTOR says nothing)* Until today I wasn't bothered about you, one way or the other. But now I do care about you. *(They embrace)* We're both strangers here.

(JABER comes back carrying a bundle of dried firewood. VICTOR and HELENA separate. VICTOR sits down, exhausted, on the ground)

VICTOR   Got to get some sleep now.

HELENA   We're in danger.

VICTOR   Got to get to sleep. The longest sleep of my life.

(JABER throws down the bundle of firewood)

JABER   Yes. That's the best way to save food and water. I'm going to sleep too.

HELENA   I don't want to die in my sleep. Let's do something.

JABER   What?

HELENA   Run.

JABER   Where?

HELENA   East or west, I don't know. Or weep. Or light a fire. Let's do something! Now!

JABER   What can we do?

HELENA   We could all shout together. Maybe someone would hear us.

JABER   Only the wind would hear you.

VICTOR   And me. You'd just stop me getting my sleep.

(HELENA walks away from them and tries to call out – but her voice comes out feebly)

HELENA   Hello! Is there anybody there?

           *(HELENA realises that her shouting seems absurdly
           weak)*

JABER   We'll light a fire when it gets dark. Stop playing the
           fool. Rest your body. Rest your head.

VICTOR   Shouting's no use.

           *(HELENA regains her courage, takes a deep breath,
           tries again)*

HELENA   Hello! Anyone there?

           *(JABER turns to VICTOR as if he likes the idea. They
           both join in the calling, desperately)*

ALL   Hello! Anyone there? *(Echo)* Hello! Anyone there?

HELENA   Just a moment. I can see something. Something
           shining.

JABER   I can't see it.

VICTOR   Where?

HELENA   Over there. Shining. It's like ... it's a river.

JABER   Stop. There's no river.

           *(But VICTOR has grabbed his hunting rifle and pack
           and is racing off towards the river he has seen)*

HELENA   Come on! Water!

VICTOR   *(off)* I can see it properly now. Water! Water!

HELENA   Water! *(HELENA grabs her pack and follows
           VICTOR).* Water!

           (JABER stands sadly. He watches them go. He sits and

watches. Suddenly he is overwhelmed by tears. He gets up. He picks up all the gear he can carry)

JABER   I'm coming. *(JABER runs after them)*

(Another part of the desert – we lose the Land Rover and see a little rocky gully. VICTOR enters, kneels and gazes)

VICTOR   Yes, I can see it. Like a waterfall gushing out of the rocks. And then it makes a river. A river running right to the horizon. Water! Water! Water!

(Enter HELENA. She clasps VICTOR's hand. They struggle over the rocks)

HELENA   Water! Water! Where is it Victor?

VICTOR   Down there. Got to climb down there. Plenty of water.

VICTOR &
HELENA   Water! Water!

HELENA   Where?

VICTOR   Here. Round here. The water. Here it is. Let's swim. *(He tears off his shirt and crawls to the edge of a rock)*

HELENA   Where's the water?

VICTOR   It's cool and good. Oh. Look out. They're coming. Keep 'em off me. Get out! They're killing me. Get off. *(HELENA watches powerlessly as VICTOR struggles with invisible attackers).* Murderers. *(VICTOR stumbles and falls)* No, don't shoot! *(VICTOR levels his rifle at his own head).* Don't shoot me. Don't shoot.

(Enter JABER, running. He drops his gear and grabs the rifle away from VICTOR)

JABER   That's enough. We'll need that.

VICTOR   He tried to shoot me.

HELENA   Jaber. Where's the Land Rover?

JABER   I don't know.

           *(VICTOR has collapsed on the ground. HELENA
           gives him her hand)*

HELENA   Come on, Victor.

VICTOR   No. I've got to sleep.

JABER   We're lost.

VICTOR   I've got to sleep.

           *(VICTOR sleeps. HELENA and JABER face each
           other. Fade down. Music. Fade up on another part of
           the desert.)*

           *(There is no Land Rover. The ground is rough with a
           number of rocky outcrops. Otherwise the stage is
           completely empty. It is shortly before sunset and the
           music continues. As the three re-emerge on to the
           stage we see that they have now rid themselves of most
           of their clothes because of the crushing heat. They are
           near collapse. They have marched for a whole day in
           the heat of the sun)*

           *(VICTOR appears, dragging himself along, his breath
           coming slowly, heavily. He is suffering from heat
           stroke. He wears jeans, with his shirt over his head
           and shoulders. As soon as he reaches the rocks, he
           collapses. It's obvious that he can't continue)*

VICTOR   God! They nearly got me. Wild bedouins on horses
           big as camels. Swords slicing the air, blinding as
           lasers. They were enjoying the hunt, screaming out
           their war-cries. *(He attempts to scream as they did)*

65

Yes, nearly got me. They just erupted out of the sand. I'd crawled as far as the river – and then a great mouth opened in the ground and spewed out this flood of crazy desert pirates and the river all dried up and they nearly got me. It was just me, alone. But Jaber, I thought you were coming to save me.

(JABER enters, carrying HELENA. He is still strong, but HELENA looks ill. Both are dressed in rags. JABER helps HELENA to support herself on a rock. They look like castaways on a savage abandoned shore)

HELENA   The world around me is full of green birds. The world around me is full of green birds. The world around me is full of green birds. Never so many green birds covering the whole world around me. Green birds blocking the windows so I can't see out. Can you see them? All round me. Uncountable spreading wings. White handkerchiefs fluttering like they came from a magician's pocket. And their song is agony.

Hurry, they sing. Thirsty, they sing. Put a little water in my right hand. *(Holds out her hand)* Put some breadcrumbs in my left hand. *(Holds out her other hand)* You can feed now. You can drink now. Oh, you're pecking my hands, but there's no bread or water. Your singing hurts me. You sing about death pains. Save me with drops of water, water, water, water.

JABER   Shouldn't have left the Land Rover. I couldn't stop you. *(Finds some desert grass and gives them each a little)* Put a little grass in your mouth. She can't hear me. Take some. *(Puts the grass in her hand and helps her to put some in her mouth)* Victor, can you hear me? It won't quench your thirst but it'll help your saliva.

VICTOR   Soon as they came out of the earth, the river dried up. I ran like a wild horse. I was alone, Helena. Scared silly. I stumbled. Rocks underfoot. I fell. Scraped the

66

skin off my knees and elbows. The horses were going to trample me. So I got up again. And ran. They'd have skinned me alive. *(Listening)* Hoofbeats. But far away. And war-cries. But in the distance, just little echoes. I've escaped.

HELENA   I want a few breadcrumbs and a little water. Then my green birds will be safe. I can't stand the sight of birds suffering. Don't let them die. Please. Don't let them die!

JABER   They'll survive. Don't worry about them, Helena. As soon as night falls, they'll flutter back to their nests.

HELENA   Can you see them, Jaber?

JABER   I can't see them now, Helena. But I know them. My whole life has been spent in the desert, so I've been honoured by their company. I remember them many years ago, when our caravan sank into the sands and all the water was gone.

HELENA   So many wings. You couldn't count them. Green handkerchiefs waving goodbye.

VICTOR   Do you know anything about those horses? I yelled out to you to come and help. You didn't hear me. Will they happen again?

JABER   Those horses have gone to pull the chariots of the sun behind the gates of the night. They won't attack again till noon tomorrow. And perhaps they won't find us here. Can you still see the river? Or are you better now?

VICTOR   I feel better. But it's a real river Jaber. I know you'll laugh at me. But the river really exists. Can't explain it, but as soon as it appears, it vanishes. But I did see it. And just a moment ago, it was here, right here, here. But it escaped. Why do rivers run away from me? Why do wild men of the desert chase me? What have I done wrong? And these horses – big as camels,

67

bigger, big as elephants, why do they chase me? I don't know. I do remember that it died. Yes, it died. They betrayed it. They plotted against the river. And then they killed it. I don't know. I don't know, the whole thing's muddled up. I don't know anything. Not any more. I just want one thing, Jaber. I want to rest. Why did you let us wander away from that house? Wander away to this land of murderers. What did they have against me? But they killed the river. And then they tried to kill me too.

JABER   Our car was the house. A little protection from the heat. I told you not to leave it. But you wouldn't listen. I told you that the desert carries whips of fire.

VICTOR   One of them took a rifle. He came over to me. He tried to blast my head off.

JABER   It was you. You aimed your rifle at your own head. The last round. If we hadn't grabbed it, you'd be dead. I don't blame you. I went through a moment like that, when suicide seems the best idea. But I fought it. I turned to Allah and asked for his help in throwing that idea away.

VICTOR   I remember now. A woman came and took my hand and I went with her.

JABER   You mean Helena?

VICTOR   I've been so stupid. I remember. I saw Helena running along shouting water, water, water.

HELENA   *(in a voice like a quiet echo)* Water, water, water.

VICTOR   Couldn't stop myself. I ran too. I saw the spring myself. Like a waterfall gushing out of the rocks and forming a river which stretched out to the horizon. And I was running too. And shouting: Water! Water! Water!

JABER   . Victor, you know it was a mirage.

68

VICTOR   Who told you it was a mirage? you didn't see it. You
              don't know. You started shouting at us: Stay where
              you are. Don't leave the shade! Don't go running after
              an illusion. And we shouted back: It's a river. Come
              and see. Come and drink the water. But you wouldn't
              understand. I was extremely surprised that somebody
              with desert experience couldn't tell the difference
              between a mirage and flowing water. I promise I saw
              the river. It really existed. I promise. I saw the river. In
              the hottest depths of an empty desert I found a spring
              of leaping water. And I was very happy.

HELENA   Won't you do anything to save these birds? If only my
              mum was here. Things would be a bit different. She
              was a wonderful mother. She'd take me by the hand
              lead me round the zoological gardens. There were
              lakes. Swans swimming on green lakes. Trees full of
              monkeys. Pigeons sat on our shoulders and our heads
              as if they'd always known us. I'd swing on the swings
              and whirl on the whirligig and go five hundred miles
              an hour down the humpback slide and then I'd ask
              mum for some old sliced bread to feed the animals and
              the birds. She was a lovely mum. If only she'd hurry
              up and come and cheer these birds up. Poor things.
              Breaks my heart, the broken-up way they sing. If
              nobody does anything they'll die pretty soon.

VICTOR   What can I do about it, now the river's dead?

JABER   Which river?

VICTOR   The river that they hate. Didn't you see them? Coming
              to the river as wild savage tribes, yelling and riding
              those malformed horses with the necks of camels.
              First thing they did they started to kill the river. And
              then it died. And the pale yellow colour of death
              engulfed and covered the whole world. And then the
              stars died. Then the trees died. And the songs and the
              grass and the butterflies and the wheat. The harvest
              season died. The springtime withered away. The dawn
              chorus stopped – sudden as a heart attack. The earth

              69

split open to swallow the city of love. And on the evening of the same day all the birds of the air committed suicide. They killed the river. And then they came to kill me. And I know that they'll try again.

HELENA   Water, water, water. Save me with a few drops of water.

JABER   I didn't think we could carry on till nightfall. I thought Helena would collapse. And then a few steps. Then you would collapse. And me last. But here we are and the page of the day has been turned. But our page has not been turned. Not yet. I never thought that hellish sun would vanish before we did. Astonishing. A beautiful young woman from the city, who's never seen a desert before, and she's showing this extraordinary ability to survive. So now we can let the soft moist breezes of the evening caress our skin, stroking away the fear of that great fire. Evening has come and the river of illusion has disappeared.

VICTOR   You don't understand. I saw the river. It really existed. I was happy.

HELENA   Why didn't we stay and have a picnic by the river, drinking each other's health in glasses of silver water?

JABER   I wish I could be like you two, and save myself by escaping into fantasies. But the desert's a cruel cage without a door. The best thing is to recite the name of Allah. It is best to prepare to meet Him. *(Murmurs a prayer)* All I miss is my children. The littlest one is Mabruk. He is three years old. He runs out of the house at dawn and doesn't come indoors again till sunset. I miss him so much that I keep shutting my eyes so I can see him. When I know I'm going away, I even miss him before I leave home. How can he face the world without me?

VICTOR   My feet are hurting. They're all swollen. As if we'd been walking on red-hot coals.

(VICTOR takes off his shoes and it's now clear that he's regaining his mental energy as the air cools. JABER continues his prayers)

JABER   It's a good sign. You're regaining consciousness.

VICTOR   I never lost it.

HELENA   I've never heard them in such pain. Yesterday they sang so sweetly. They sounded like the happiest creatures in the world. I was sitting and drinking in the shadow of a wood. Roses and dog-daisies and streams all around me and a candle nearby with butterflies hovering round it. The dusk was all grainy, but I saw him, all bright in his sailor's uniform. And I rushed to him and we threw our arms around each other and we rolled together on the grass. And there we lay until late into the night. And when the moon came up we walked over the mossy stones down to the river. We stole a fishing boat. I lay my head on his chest and the boat gradually moved along the water. And he sang to me. He sang:

(Sings)   Where are you going, my golden girl?
              Where are you going today?

JABER   We should have stayed by the Land Rover. We should have kept her there.

VICTOR   We couldn't have spent our last moments helpless and chained to the steel side of that Land Rover. You couldn't have forced us both to stay.

JABER   We could have avoided walking in that killing glare. We might have lasted another day or two. We must be being made to suffer for some sin we've committed. Oh, Lord of the Universe! We beg for your pardon and your mercy!

VICTOR   For God's sake, forget the bloody Land Rover. Let the sand bury it. We drank all the water. Nearly poisoned

71

ourselves drinking the radiator dry. We've shouted all day and night till our throats are full of blisters. We burned everything inflammable to attract attention at night. But the world closed its ears and its eyes.

JABER It was funny about that plane. When we thought it had come to rescue us. And we all hugged each other and cheered. But he flew on and on.

VICTOR And we didn't know that we were the victims of some great conspiracy.

JABER Yes, an international conspiracy. Got up by the oil companies. Why didn't they line the desert with garages? So all you could do was to try and save yourself with your hunting rifle?

VICTOR Helena was brighter than me. What else can we do now that our lips and tongues and throats are slitting with thirst. There's nothing else to do except run in search of that river.

HELENA Where are you going, my golden girl?
Where are you going today?

JABER The river was fever. Madness.

VICTOR Nobody forced you to come with us.

JABER She's so young. And I had to watch her run over the desert screaming with joy because she'd found water. When I saw that the black birds of sadness settled in my heart. I felt guilty. Because I couldn't do anything. I saw her running and she was happy and the tears poured from my eyes. And I decided to stay where I was by the car. But when I saw both of you running away over the dunes, this feeling of fear and loneliness came over me. For the first time I thought about death. I realised that I would have to face it in this barren place alone. And the next thing I was racing behind you and running as if a lion was after me.

HELENA   Where are you going, my golden girl?
            Where are you going today?

VICTOR   Tired of running. Worn out by running. Time to stop
            running.

JABER   There's only one consolation. Everything in the world
            which has a beginning must also have an end.

VICTOR   Tell you what hurts me, Jaber. All my life has been
            spent bloody running. I've never really rested for one
            day. I've never let myself enjoy the world. I've never
            enjoyed the most basic things – like sitting with a
            family by a fire. Of chatting away an evening with
            friends over a bottle. It was all business, running
            business, work, running work, running, running and
            kidding myself I was doing it for my own future. I
            forgot that life's like a watch – it can stop any
            moment. I was planning to build an ideal house, the
            house of a lifetime! Lifetime? Stupid! I was going to
            build it near Los Angeles, near the beach, overlooking
            the Pacific, a place where most people are in the
            movie business. I bought the land. I drew up plans for
            the house. I was going to have a pool with multi-
            coloured fish and white statues all round the garden.
            And grass, deep green grass, proper English grass, not
            that spiky Californian stuff like dwarf cactuses. But
            that house of a lifetime is tens of thousands of miles
            away and I've spent my lifetime on oil and now my
            time is up and my Land Rover's died of no petrol and
            I'm dying of no water. My lifetime's drying up inside
            me. Who'd have thought I'd die without a grave or a
            coffin, or roses? Nobody's going to cry for me. What
            a miserable stupid thing to happen.

JABER   Put your faith in these rocks. Believe in these rocks.
            We may have to seek their protection from the heat of
            tomorrow.

VICTOR   We've walked far enough. I can't face the heat of
            another day. Jaber, the whole world's just a

confidence trick.

JABER   Maybe tomorrow morning these rocks will cast a little
            shadow. Enough for our three heads. How's Helena?

VICTOR   Helena, are you all right? *(VICTOR feels HELENA's
            forehead)* The air is cold, but she's still got a fever.
            She needs a doctor.

HELENA   Where are you going, my golden girl?
            Where are you going today?
            We've been going for a long, long time. And now
            we're here. Time to take the packs off our backs.
            Heavy, they're so heavy! Let's lay them down. Then
            we'll be free. Give me your hand, Victor.

JABER   If only you'd come back to the Land Rover when I
            begged you to. We could be lying in the shade on
            mattresses suitable for dying. What's the use, Victor?
            Now I understand. I'm the one all this is meant for. So
            many times the desert has trapped me and then let me
            go. But I knew some day that the desert would take
            me. I knew that after spending so many years on my
            education, the desert wouldn't let me abandon it.
            When I made up my mind to go to work in the city, I
            knew it was futile. The desert had decided that I
            should read its book and drink its glass and learn
            where it hides its gazelles.

            I was sick of the desert. I admit it. It was strange and
            treacherous and I ran away from it. But as soon as I
            found myself surrounded by four walls, my chest
            began to tighten up and I'd do anything to get back to
            the only place where I could breathe properly. I used
            to get together with some friends and we'd stage
            camel races. I won most of the time. Well, it wasn't
            me who won. It was Garzeel. My camel. He was so
            quick-tempered that my friends called him Garzeel
            after a cruel desert god who's like a bull. Garzeel was
            an extraordinary camel. If he ever lost a race he would
            crouch down and sulk and refuse all food and drink
            until he'd won a race. When I won I used to ride

Garzeel over the dunes, and I felt like the king of the whole world. But Garzeel felt like the king of the universe. There was a warm friendship between me and that camel. And between me and the desert. The three of us became one.

When the night comes, the desert changes completely. I hate the desert in the daytime. I love it in the night. I would be utterly alone in the desert, looking forward to the night when I'd light a fire as big as a castle that would burn away all my loneliness. Reclining on the ground and drinking cups of tea and considering the stars.

I used to try to number them and, because there were far more than I could count, I felt a joy inside me. It was good to think that I was the only one brave enough to ride out into this emptiness to count the stars. And I would stay awake counting them until I fell asleep still counting. Watching the galaxies, I learned their friendships and their footpaths. And all next day I would be waiting for their reappearance so I could continue. And after a few nights I completed my counting. So now the desert can do what it likes with me. Let the curse of the gazelles descend upon me. It can strike me with the whips of the sun and drive me out to be swallowed by the vast wilderness. But the desert gave me everything. The strength of my body. The meaning of my life. And so now the desert comes and asks for me. I would have preferred a little more time, a period of grace, instead of this frontal assault, but ... I am the one all this is meant for ... nobody else but me.

HELENA   My eyes won't open. Trying as hard as I can but they won't. You two, you're just blurry shapes.

JABER   That's a good sign. I think you're getting better now.

HELENA   Where are you going, my golden girl?
              Where are you going today?

VICTOR	Yesterday I saw a vision. A vision in a dream.
JABER	It was the right thing to do. We saw you fall asleep. We really envied you, Helena and I. You managed to conquer your pain with sleep. Neither of us could sleep at all.
VICTOR	I lost consciousness. I saw a dream. I saw you, Jaber. You stood up from the place where you were lying. You lay down next to Helena. I saw you in the dream. You asked her to make love with you. At first she turned away from you. But then, in the dream, I saw that she surrendered. And she made love to you. Next morning I woke up with my dream. I was disgusted with myself. And I found the world disgusting. But now everything is different. Jaber, this last day has crawled by like a year. *(He turns towards HELENA who is groaning weakly)* Helena, what's wrong? Where does it hurt? Helena!
HELENA	A bottomless well. I was falling into a bottomless well. Falling and falling but it was bottomless. Horrible dream.

(VICTOR presses her hand)

JABER	Victor. Helena loves you. What happened happened against our will. The night was very long. We thought we would die in the desert. And we had not learned to live with this idea, like we have now. So we were filled with terror. You conquered your fear with sleep. We tried to conquer ours with sex. Don't judge us too badly, Victor. Even as you slept, Helena did not take her eyes away from you. Even as we lay in each other's arms she spoke of nothing but you. I became sure that this woman loves you.
HELENA	Where are you going, my golden girl? Where are you going today? Are you still there, Victor?
VICTOR	I'm here, Helena. Beside you.

HELENA   Do you know where we are?

VICTOR   Yes, I know. We'll get through. Everything's going to
          be all right.

HELENA   There's a stone weighing down on my head. There's a
          black bandage pressing against my eyes. You know
          those green birds who were hovering round me? One
          by one they're dropping to the ground from thirst and
          the heat of the sun. They've all died now. Victor, I'm
          frightened.

VICTOR   Don't be frightened, Helena. We've got the best guide
          in the Sahara. He knows the desert like the back of his
          hand and he eats snakes for breakfast.

          (JABER tries to laugh)

HELENA   All the green birds have died. I'm scared. Please don't
          go away. Please don't leave me to die.

VICTOR   Helena, don't talk like that. Don't talk like that. We're
          here with you. We're going to win through. All I want
          in the world is to be with you. We're never going to be
          apart. I want to be with you always because I love
          you, Helena. You are beautiful and noble and delicate
          and brave. And I love you, Helena.

          *(HELENA raises her head and stares fixedly at him.
          She puts her arms round his neck as if she had just
          discovered him)*

HELENA   But I don't want to die! I don't want to die! Victor, I
          don't want to die. *(She weeps)*

VICTOR   Those moments. Those moments outside and beyond
          all laws of time and space. Those amazing moments
          when I was chasing that gazelle, with no will or mind
          of my own. It was like being moved by unknown
          forces. I remember. I looked and the gazelle was
          leading me towards the source of all light, towards a

new, strange land. There were islands of red coral. A shining archipelago. And the islands were roofed over by a sky of brilliant colours. And there was a scent of roses and there was the sound of singing. I saw a great eternal celebration, like a wedding, and I saw souls like glowing apples and I saw men who shone like water. And so I drove into the black zone. It was all my fault. You shouldn't have suffered. I risked your lives. It was me, not the petrol, not the Land Rover. I'm sorry.

HELENA   Where are you going, my golden girl?
           Where are you going today?
           I am going on board the golden ship ...
           (She can't remember the last line)

JABER   Not your fault. It's the god Garzeel. After they struck oil in the desert, he began to be as moody as the God of the Nile who used to demand a bride every springtime as a sacrifice in return for general fertility. Helena is a bride being offered to Garzeel so he will allow money to flower from the desert.

HELENA   Where are you going, my golden girl?
           Where are you going today?
           I am going on board the golden ship
           That waits ...

VICTOR   But he could have taken anyone. Why Helena?

JABER   It's the wrong time to ask.

HELENA   You know, I'm longing to see Agamemnon. I want to stroke his head and his back and down along his tail. His ears fold flat when you stroke his head, he likes them folding flat. I want to hold him close to my face and sing to him, sing to him. I wonder if we've got there yet.

VICTOR   Everything will be fine.

HELENA   That gazelle we were chasing came to visit me. From

78

round its neck she took a jewelled necklace and hung it round my neck. And then I knew she was my friend.

VICTOR   That's a good gazelle. Jaber, I want to ask you something.

JABER   No more questions.

VICTOR   I want to ask you for something. Please don't let me down.

JABER   I won't let you down.

VICTOR   Leave us here. Now. Just go ahead. Carry on as far as you can.

HELENA   Where are you going, my golden girl?

JABER   But that ...

VICTOR   *(Interrupting)* Don't argue. Get going. Neither of us is strong enough to walk. You walk, for both of us. Carry a message from me and from her. Then, if you get through, you'll give some sort of meaning to all our suffering. Helena going to find the river won't be in vain. It won't seem absurd that she gave us the good news of finding water. You'll give a meaning to our battle against thirst and the desert. So thirst and the desert won't win, not completely. Go on. Get going.

JABER   Don't talk like that. It's no good.

VICTOR   Now's your chance. You'll find your way through the silence of the night to the barking of a dog carried by the breeze. By some miracle like that you'll win through.

HELENA   Where are you going, my golden girl?
         Where are you going today?
         I am going on board the golden ship
         That waits in the Golden Bay.

JABER	There are no barking dogs. Not within two day's walking. I couldn't walk for more than two hours. For the love of Allah let me pass my last moments here.
VICTOR	You've got nothing to lose. You'll be doing it for all of us, won't you? Let's keep fighting till the end.
JABER	Victor, you're talking like a general on the battlefield. It's stupid for me to go out into the blazing heat of another day. I want to die with my head in the shade. And I won't leave Helena in this state.
VICTOR	What can you do for her? Look, suppose you find a caravan or a hunter or even a stray camel. You might be able to save us too. Go on. Now.
JABER	But ...
VICTOR	Every moment counts. Please. Go now.
JABER	You're forcing me.
VICTOR	You promised not to let me down. Here's your stick.

(A moment of silence)

JABER	First I want to say goodbye to Helena.
HELENA	Where are you going, my golden girl? Where are you going today?

(JABER kisses HELENA on her forehead. He grips VICTOR by the shoulder and holds out his hand to him. They shake hands. VICTOR takes a wallet from his pocket)

VICTOR	My wallet. Take it with you.

(JABER takes it and makes as if to leave. As he is about to go he stops. The lights begin to dim)

HELENA   Please don't leave me all alone. I want to go out for a walk with Agamemnon. I want you both to take me to Agamemnon.

(JABER goes back to where he was. He throws away his stick and remains standing)

JABER   I've decided not to go.

(JABER hands over the wallet to VICTOR, who throws it down carelessly by his side)

VICTOR   Why?

JABER   No questions. I'm not going. That's all.

VICTOR   A moment ago –

JABER   *(Interrupting in a calm voice)* What right have you to dictate to me now? I'm staying here. I will die here. Alongside you and Helena.

VICTOR   If I die now, I've got an excuse. Thirst killed me. But you're just dying for your own meaningless pride.

(Moments pass and then JABER throws himself down in his place by the rock)

JABER   I thought of the shame that would fall on my children when the people of my village learnt that I was a guide who left my companions in their distress and went to try and save myself. *(Silence)* And now the night has come. So let me have the pleasure of reclining here, observing the stars and praising God until sleep comes to me.

(Silence)

VICTOR   Yes, count the stars. Then you can be sure they're all still there for whoever inherits this sky from you.

(Silence)

JABER   Yes, I will count the stars so long as I'm sure that a
             beautiful death is approaching.

             (Silence)

VICTOR   That picture you drew us of Paradise. Is it true that in
             Paradise a man always stays young and handsome?

JABER   Of course. *(Silence)* Otherwise it wouldn't be
             Paradise. *(Silence)* I will praise Allah that when my
             end has come I show obedience to Him and bear
             witness that there is no God but God.

             *(HELENA suddenly gets to her feet and takes a few
             steps forward. She looks left and right with her eyes
             closed, trying to walk forward. Then she turns back,
             but is unable to walk. It is hard to stay standing. She
             falls to the ground.*

             *JABER goes to help her. He supports her from one
             side, VICTOR from the other. The three of them stand
             in the centre of the stage with their backs to the
             audience while the lights continue to dim)*

HELENA   *(Sings in a weak voice)* Where are you going, my
             golden girl?
             Where are you going today?
             I am going on board the golden ship.

JABER   I think she's going now. *(He murmurs prayers to
             himself)*

VICTOR   I wish I could do something. Helena? Can you feel
             anything? She can't hear me. She's moved away from
             us now. But she can't feel any pain, Jaber, that's the
             important thing. She sings and she's happy.

HELENA   Where are you going, my golden girl?
             Where are you going today?

             (JABER and VICTOR join her in singing while the

82

darkness grows more intense and they appear only as silhouettes, singing in weak voices)

ALL   Where are you going, my golden girl?
Where are you going today?
I am going on board the golden ship
That waits in the Golden Bay.

(At the very edge of the stage we see a small spot of light like the light of a match while the song continues. Only JABER stops singing to comment on it as the others continue to sing)

JABER   I think I can see a small speck of light. Can you see it too, Victor?

(The stage is illuminated. JABER, VICTOR and HELENA collapse gradually in silence. Lights begin to dim. As the stage darkens, gazelles advance and stand around the three corpses)

CURTAIN

HAROLD

(Office. A man at his desk reading newspaper which obscures his face. Knock on door, enter HAROLD)

MAN   *(Without lifting head, face still hidden)* Sit down, Harold.

HAROLD   Sir, I'm sorry, sir, er ...

MAN   Don't be. No need to be. Sit down, Harold.

HAROLD   Perhaps you are confusing me with some other person – my name is actually Allen.

MAN   *(Putting away paper)* Come on, Harold. Why do you say such a thing? Your name is not Allen, it's Harold, it has always been Harold. There's nothing wrong with the name Harold. Don't ever try to apologise for it – on the contrary, you should always be proud of such a name. There was once a King with the name Harold. So please don't try to run away from your own name.

HAROLD   But I – I can't be mistaken about my name, I'm sure of it. No-one has ever called me Harold except for you, sir, and you've only met me for the first time. I don't even have a friend or a relative by the name of Harold. You must have got me mixed up with some other chap. I can prove that my name is Allen. *(Puts hand in pocket searching for cards)*

MAN   No need for that, Harold, no need at all. *(Paternal tone)* I know perfectly well that your name is Harold, and you are not going to change it by standing up to me like that, pretending that your name is Allen!

(In a more formal tone) Sit down, Harold.

HAROLD   *(Shrugs, puzzled)* Oh, well, if that's the way you want it – let it be so – Harold it is.

(Hands him the papers he brought with him and sits)

MAN   *(Examining the papers)* I understand you've come to me about the job.

HAROLD   Yes, sir.

MAN   And you were sent by ...?

HAROLD   Roger Davies of ...

MAN   *(interrupting)* Yes, yes.

HAROLD   They thought I was fit for the job, so they sent me for your approval.

MAN   Have you been made aware of the hazards this job involves?

HAROLD   To me it is not a job, sir. Diving has always been a pleasure – my favourite sport, since I was a boy. All I have ever wanted to do with my life is to dive.

MAN   How very charming; how very impressive; how very pleasant. It always gives me the utmost satisfaction to meet people like you, people with hearts full of love for England, ready to go and dive for their country ...

HAROLD   *(Not sure whether he said die or dive)*

MAN   Dive, I said.

HAROLD   But I'm not English, sir. I happen to be Irish. I hope that doesn't affect the situation as it stands now ...?

MAN   Of course not. It's even better. It gives me even more pleasure to see Irish men with their hearts full of love for England ready to go to the North Sea and dive for it!

86

HAROLD	*(Not sure)* Yes ... sir.
MAN	We must always look for brave and courageous young men like yourself, keen on diving for their country. We have to keep the recruitment flowing. *(Sinister voice)* And, as you know, that's because we do tend to lose them from time to time ... Tragic ... is it not? *(Hands him the papers back)* Well ... you have my approval. Give this to the man next door – he will take care of the rest.
HAROLD	When can I start?
MAN	Any time from now on – the sooner the better, of course. Goodbye!
HAROLD	*(Mutters unintelligible words, walks towards the door)*
MAN	Harold.
HAROLD	Yes.
MAN	Why did you lie to me?
HAROLD	*(Looks at him in astonishment)*
MAN	Why did you say your name was Allen when it was Harold?
HAROLD	*(On the verge of tears)* But it's Allen, sir, have one of my cards – what else can I do to prove it? That's my identification card! – my national health card! – my club card – my bus pass, my train pass ... Allen ... Allen ... Allen ...
	(Throws them on the table in front of the man)
MAN	*(Looks at the cards, then back at Harold)* It's Harold.
HAROLD	*(In horror, takes one of the cards, examines it.*

Examines his photo on card.) It's impossible! Just impossible!

(In horror takes another card and examines it) This one's Harold too!

(Takes cards one after another) Harold ... Harold ... Harold ... Harold ... *(Voice becoming hoarse)* I can't breathe ... I can't breathe ...

CURTAIN

THE EVENING VISITOR

ELIZABETH   *A lady in her fifties*

DONALD   *A man in his forties*

MARTHA   *The maid, a young woman*

Scene (Luxurious drawing room, Evening, and a beam of yellow departing sun coming through an open window – back stage, where the garden appears flourishing and rosey. When the curtain opens, we see the maid emptying the ashtrays and singing to herself.)

MAID
You eagle
High you go up
High you fly
Won't you lend me your wings
To say a little prayer
To my dearest man
In his highest
In his place of shadow and light.

LADY
(Coming through a door at the left)
You keep on singing to your admirable little man, forgetting to put the lights on as you were ordered. Don't worry, you needn't go up to him; he's already half way through coming down to you ... The spring's sun must have dissolved the wintery cloud that was his refuge, and we will soon hear his splash down ... on the roof of my house ... perhaps.

(She puts on the light)

MAID
The sun hasn't gone down yet ... madam ... we may, just as well, wait a bit longer till it's dark ...

LADY
Oh ... Martha ... it is an anticipation of the dark ... just a precautionary step. I feel obliged to take before its

attack. I am so frightened of the dark today, Martha. The sun will soon depart into the salty waters of the sea ... and the ancient animal is awakened then ... so all the lights must be on before it comes creeping into my house, flooding us with the black air it breathes ... *(Silence)* Martha ... don't forget to light the Christmas tree too ...

MAID   What did you say madam ... did you mention the Christmas tree?

LADY   Light it ... Martha.

MAID   But Christmas is far away ahead ... or rather far away behind.

LADY   I just like to see it lit tonight Martha ... don't be so noisy ...

MAID   Whatever you say madam. *(Leaves kitchen from side door)*

LADY   *(Goes towards the vase of flowers on the table and checks it)* Martha ... have you seen the flowers I picked from the garden today?

MAID   They are here in the kitchen.

LADY   Bring them in here.

(Martha brings the Christmas Tree and the flowers, the lady takes the flowers, then looks at the tree)

LADY   It needs dusting.

(Lady goes to arrange the flowers, the maid starts dusting the tree)

MAID   *(While dusting the tree)* He will soon give his usual knock ... the same time ...

LADY   Yes he will ... as soon as the sun goes down, he turns up ...

MAID   With the twilight he comes ... he never misses his time ... the same knock ... the same time ...

LADY   *(Looking away)* He never fears the dark ...

MAID   Perhaps he fears the sunlight.

LADY   He must be tired of knocking on our door by now.

MAID   He never uses the bell, I wonder why ... He just knocks, so gently and smoothly ... tap ... tap ... tap in rhythmical order.

LADY   He used to play piano. *(A little pause)* His playing was so fascinating, that girls were going mad about him.

MAID   Three ... He never knocks more than three times. When he hears no response, he turns back ... leaving a strange silence behind him. I could even hear his steps fading away in the distance.

LADY   He's old enough not to knock four ... *(said briskly)*

MAID   I always thought of him as a young lad ... young and handsome with curly hair ... In spite of what I hear of him, I have got a very lovely image of him, my lady.

LADY   He is much older than what you think of him ... Everyday I read what the stars tell about his horoscope in the evening paper. And that is my only source of information about him ... From this I know perfectly well what he is up to and what he is going through ...

MAID   It has been almost a year since he started coming to our door and since then he never failed to give his everyday knock; even in the peak of winter-rain and snow, he never ceased to come ... He came and knocked ... It's taken a talent to do it as steadily as he does ...

LADY	Don't forget that he is a man of talent ... Martha.
MAID	Have you read what the stars tell about him today?
LADY	Not yet ...
MAID	*(Picks up newspaper from a table nearby)* What month? What month?
LADY	April ...
MAID	What day?
LADY	You've got so interested in him ... Leave the paper ... and light the tree ...
MAID	It won't take a minute ... what day?
LADY	The fourteenth.
MAID	*(Looks at the paper)* Lady ... isn't it today the fourteenth of April?
LADY	*(With surprise)* What are you saying?
MAID	Yes ... it's today ... *(Looks at the calendar)* Today is the fourteenth of April *(happily)* So it is his birthday ... His birthday ... My lady.
LADY	*(After a pause)* I felt it ... somehow I felt it ... subconsciously I was aware of it.
MAID	So ... He won't come today ... We will miss his usual knock on the door.
LADY	Why?... What makes you think that he won't come today?
MAID	Surely he will be celebrating his birthday party somewhere. He won't have time to come here,

92

knowing that no one will open the door for him and say Happy Birthday to You ... at least ...

LADY   He will be here exactly on time Martha ... So put the kettle on the fire, and arrange the table for the evening High Tea ... I feel that he is going to be our guest tonight.

MAID   Do you mean that you're going to allow him in if he comes? Please don't take the risk, my Lady, you know how dangerous he is ...

LADY   He doesn't come to ask for trouble. He asks for a refuge.

MAID   But how can you shelter such a criminal, wanted by the Legal authorities? You've got your good name and the name of your dead husband to protect. You've got the orphan societies that you run to look after ... Think of the great damage he will bring to your prestige and social position. Don't forget your big responsibilities.

LADY   Yes, indeed, it is high time to remember my responsibilities.

MAID   And there is another thing ... if you open the door for him today, he will never come and knock again ... Life would be unbearable without his knock ... it has become part of the rituals of our evenings; it adds colour and flavour to our everyday life ... Can you imagine an evening to pass without his gentle knock on our door? You're not sacrificing that too ...

LADY   He will give it up if he gets no reply after a whole year.

MAID   No my lady ... he enjoys it ... I am sure he does ... it has become the habit he loves most and cares about, and he will never give it up ... It won't do him any good opening the door; on the contrary, it will hurt him ... so don't interfere with the course of nature.

	Let him come, give the daily intimate knock, and go. For there was no point in keeping him out for the whole year, if you are going to let him in just now ...
LADY	I have to, Martha. He cannot be kept out just for the fun of it ...
MAID	You have to ... and if he doesn't come today? If he goes celebrating his birthday somewhere else?
LADY	He will come and celebrate it here. For he knows that this is the day I must open the door for him.
MAID	Does he threaten you?
LADY	He will be our guest for high tea tonight. Bring the silver cups instead of the usual. Let him see we are hospitable. Make it look as pleasant as it can be ...

(Maid lights the tree ... goes to the kitchen ... the lady takes the paper, and reads it ... the maid returns)

MAID	I put the kettle on the fire ... What are you reading? His fortune, my lady?
LADY	It's time to take your leave ... Martha ...
MAID	I've got to be here my lady, to open the door for him ... to serve him the tea ...
LADY	I will open the door and show him in myself.
MAID	But my lady.
LADY	Go back home ... Martha.
MAID	Just to have a look at him.
LADY	You will see him later on ... Martha.
MAID	But I have no other place to go to ... my lady ... this is the only place I know ...

LADY   I have to be alone with him ... Martha ... *(takes some money from her purse)* ... That will help you to find a shelter for tonight ...

MAID   Shall I come in the morning?

LADY   Come whenever you like ... Martha ...

                (Lady turns her back ... Martha leaves the room, takes her coat and bag ... and leaves ... The sun already departed now ... Lady lights a cigarette ... checks the flowers and the Christmas tree ... then sits down and starts reading the paper after a while she hears the usual knock ...)

                (Lady goes out of stage to an inside door ... we hear)

MAN'S
VOICE   Good evening ... Elizabeth ...

LADY'S
VOICE   Good evening ... Donald ...

                (They appear both on stage ... the man in his forties ... very well built ... neatly dressed ... and carrying a DEAD bunch of flowers)

ELIZABETH   You have grown old ... your hair has become grey ...

DONALD   You are much the same ... Elizabeth ...

ELIZABETH   I am an aged and lonely woman ...

DONALD   But the glow in your face is still the same ... Elizabeth ...

ELIZABETH   Are they after you?

DONALD   Who?

ELIZABETH   The people who are after you ...

DONALD   I scare them away.

ELIZABETH   Aren't you tired of this unpleasant game?

DONALD   I do it well ... so I can never grow tired of it ... even
            when I was a child, and when we used to play hide-
            and-seek ... I was gifted in finding the securest place
            to hide in ...

ELIZABETH   Why did you come?

DONALD   As I was passing by, I thought I'd better drop in to
            say Happy Birthday to you ... *(He gives her the bunch
            of dead flowers...)* Happy Birthday to you my dear
            old lady.

ELIZABETH   *(Taking the flowers ...)* Happy Birthday to you too ...
            the flowers reveal that the visit was intended ...

DONALD   *(Interrupting)* It's spring outside my dear lady ... the
            flowers are everywhere. I took no pain in picking
            them just outside your house ...

ELIZABETH   Thanks all the same ... *(puts the flowers in the vase
            in lieu of the fresh ones already there)* It seems that
            you waited so long ...

DONALD   Oh ... the function of waiting I do with a highly
            efficient skill, since the day I was employed.

ELIZABETH   You have always been a difficult child.

DONALD   You used to be an open door to me ...

ELIZABETH   But you went away ... you grew wild ... condemned
            by everyone. The news of the murders you
            committed are in every paper ... You're wanted ...
            wanted ... wanted ...

DONALD   *(Laughing)* That is better than being unwanted ...

ELIZABETH You've been in jail many times ...

DONALD And I broke out of them many times ... too ...

ELIZABETH Innocent people *(pause)* You killed them ... *(Pause)* They were innocent ...

DONALD While you were here giving charities to the Orphan Societies.

ELIZABETH You were out there murdering the happiness of innocent people ...

DONALD And you were here taking good care of the business of your dead husband.

ELIZABETH I fear you Donald.

DONALD Fear no one ... as long as the business is prosperous.

ELIZABETH Innocent people they were ...

DONALD No one is innocent.

ELIZABETH The orphans are innocent *(pause)*. You were an orphan yourself ... You were six-days old when you were first brought to me ... You conquered my heart as a child, so I put you on my lap ... I gave you my breasts ... I fostered you and fed you till you became big ...

DONALD And then you asked me to go ... You put me in a stormy sea and you said 'Go Sailing' ...

ELIZABETH That was when you arrived the age of weaning ...

DONALD As I was sailing under your own flag ... the whole voyage was just a picnic.

ELIZABETH Your great ambition was to conquer the world ...

DONALD No matter what I conquered as long as I was busy

out there recruiting new orphans everyday for your Orphan Asylum ... just to keep you going ...

ELIZABETH   I never thought you would go as wild as that ...

DONALD   You're not going to get away with it no matter what you thought of me, Elizabeth, for you know just as much as I do that I was out there doing exactly what you wanted me to do ... fulfilling the task you prepared me for ... And whenever I did something, I was thinking of you, reading with great pleasure, the news of it in the papers, knowing that I was doing it on behalf of you ...

ELIZABETH   There is no proof of what you said ... As a widow of a knighted man, I've always tried to live up to the good name of my dead husband ... and lead an honest and honourable life ...

DONALD   And make the business prosper under your chairmanship ...

ELIZABETH   And spread joy and comfort amongst unfortunate people ...

DONALD   Among ordinary widows of ordinary men ...

(Kettle whistles ...)

ELIZABETH   Time for high tea ... *(Leaves to the kitchen to prepare tea ...)*

(DONALD goes to the record-player, puts on a record of modern beat ... starts dancing ... ELIZABETH enters with a tray containing tea-pot, two silver cups ... and two pieces of cake ... fills a cup for DONALD and another for herself)

ELIZABETH   *(While giving the cup to DONALD)* Martha forgot to bring the candles for the Birthday cake ... Anyhow, Happy returns.

98

DONALD   Thanks all the same. Happy Birthday to you too ...
            By the way, Elizabeth, you must have written your
            will by now ...

ELIZABETH   Why? ... Why do you ask Donald?

DONALD   I just thought it was wise to remind you of the will ...
            You have arrived at the age when people usually
            write their wills ...

ELIZABETH   Is that what you came here for? ...

DONALD   I am here just for the sake of making you happy ...

ELIZABETH   But you are not staying ... Are you ?

DONALD   You know perfectly well that I cannot stay here ...

ELIZABETH   You are here to stay, Donald. They are looking for
            you ... They will pick you up ... they will take you to
            jail again and they will beat you up even ...

DONALD   I am not staying, and you know it. I came just to
            remind you of the will ... I have duties to perform
            after I've done with the one here ...

ELIZABETH   You mustn't go, Donald ...

DONALD   I must go, Elizabeth ...

ELIZABETH   Why must you? ... Is it an appointment? ...

DONALD   Well ... It is an appointment ...

ELIZABETH   Where about? ...

DONALD   Not far away ...

ELIZABETH   With whom?

DONALD   A person you don't know ...

ELIZABETH What is the name of the person? ...

DONALD   Oh ... stop being annoying ...

ELIZABETH Asking a girl out? ... Are you not? Dating her. Are
          you not? ... inviting her for a dinner and dance, and
          the rest of it ... are you not? ...

DONALD   You always think in terms of young lovers ... that's
          your weak point, Elizabeth ...

ELIZABETH You have, indeed, run out of hand ... A girl ... and
          what girl? ... She must be young ... How young? ...
          Fifteen ... Fourteen perhaps; preferably blonde ... or
          just an outstanding beauty ... as you call it ... And
          where will you take her tonight? ... Danube
          Restaurant. If I may say ... the securest place in
          town for a man on the run ... where the lights are
          dim, under which your features will get nobler ...
          And in a very dignified manner, you will ask for a
          bottle of champagne and caviar, that matches your
          occasion ... The ice-cream girl will melt under your
          generosity and magnetism ... And what comes after
          is a dance ... we all know what a brilliant dancer you
          are ... We know you love it slow ... So be careful
          with the breast of the little child, don't break her
          chest, for the evening is not over yet ... still you have
          to take her to bed. And after you're arrived at the
          peak of your satisfaction, nothing will be left but to
          ask the usual question about her last wish ... and
          before you know the answer ... you stretch your
          arms, and your fingers go round her small neck ...
          and so mercilessly ... so savagely you strangle her ....
          Am I wrong?... Mr Donald?

          (She weeps loudly ...)

DONALD   These are bad symptoms of a dangerous illness. But
          you know I've never acted as a free agent ... I've
          always served your wishes with a blind obedience ...

ELIZABETH So don't go ... Stay here ... stop wandering around ...

murdering innocent people ...

DONALD   I cannot be kept indoors. My only enjoyment in life is to be in the open air ... performing my duties ...

ELIZABETH Spreading death ...

DONALD   And comfort ...

ELIZABETH Can't you stop it? ...

DONALD   No ... I can't stop it, Elizabeth ...

ELIZABETH Aren't you trying? ...

DONALD   No use trying, I arrived to the point of no return ...

          (ELIZABETH stops crying) ...

DONALD   *(After a pause ...)* Elizabeth?

ELIZABETH Yes Donald ...

DONALD   Wipe your tears ...

ELIZABETH *(Dries her tears ... and says nothing ...)*

DONALD   And now Elizabeth ...

ELIZABETH Now what?

DONALD   *(Stands up ...)* Let's get down to work ... *(ELIZABETH stands up trembling ... and trying to walk backward ...)*

DONALD   Come here Elizabeth ... (She doesn't move ... He goes towards her ...) Tell me now Elizabeth ... *(Stretches his arms and puts his fingers around her neck ...)*

          WHAT IS YOUR LAST WISH? ...
          (Scream fading out ... with curtain falling down...)

THE SINGING OF THE STARS
A One-Act Play

SETTING: (Open ground unbounded except by the horizon. A lean, lonely tree, with dry leaves, whose trunk is full of protuberances and burns, occupies C, with a swing made of bed linen hanging down from its dry branches. Nearby there is a motor cycle and a man and a woman wearing safari dress, co-operating in folding a safari bed, which they had been using for sleeping. Around them are plates, tissue papers and other articles used in picnics. They are talking as they collect their things and making ready to leave the place, after they had spent the night under the tree. Each of them keeps a cup of tea-and-milk aside and goes back to it every now and then. They use the swing sometimes. It is morning.)

MAN   *(Putting the folded bed in the part used for luggage at the back of the motor cycle, goes back to take a sip from the cup of tea which he had put aside, then takes a card box, opens it and picks up a piece of tart using a fork)*

Come and taste it, dear. It is still delicious. Very delicious. I thought that leaving this tart for a whole night would make it go off.

(The woman draws near, and he puts the piece in her mouth)

WOMAN   It won't go off even if it remained there for a whole week because the air here is free from the pollution which poisons food as well as human life. See how one wakes up full of energy, joy, refreshment and love of life.

(She opens up her arms, inhaling and exhaling the air)

I shall store in my body an extra amount of the fresh air, to help me live in the polluted environment of the

103

city. I've never slept so beautifully in my life as I did last night. I had pleasant dreams. Shall I tell you something and promise me you won't laugh.

MAN   Say it, say it and don't ever remain silent, but don't prevent me from laughing. With you I want to laugh, play, let myself go and release all the charges of chagrin, pain and depression which weighed on my chest before I met you.

WOMAN   Would you believe me if I say that last night I imagined I heard the singing of the stars and that their singing was beautiful.

MAN   Of course I believe you. Human life on earth couldn't possibly have continued without the guidance of the stars which take care of it from the cradle to the grave. And whom should the stars sing to if not for a woman like you who shines and twinkles as they do in the night.

WOMAN   The tune was full of joy, and the stars were singing to me of love, calling me to be their guest, wishing to feed me from their divine banquets and offer me a drink of their heavenly light. I'll try to recall the tune. It was something like this.

(She hums the tune laughing, as she dances and claps her hand. The man participates in the clapping and the dancing and reiterates the tune with her. Then they laugh, fall in each other's embrace and separate.)

WOMAN   How beautiful this open ground is which seems as if it has slipped from human memory and nobody cared to inhabit it, and has remained in its pristine state since the early beginnings of the universe. We must come back to this place once again.

MAN   The credit goes to you for hitting upon it. You, who always refused to go to hotels or to stay inside houses and wanted us to go out and spend the night in the middle of naked nature.

WOMAN   I wanted the adventure to be complete. An adventure
         in love as well as an adventure in time and place. Our
         emotional adventure would be lacking without adding
         to it the adventure of escaping with our love to nature, ⌐
         which does not wear any dress or wear any colour
         other than the colours of earth and sky.

MAN   It was a stroke of good luck that the weather was just
         fine all the time.

WOMAN   Even if it had been cold and stormy, it wouldn't have
         diminished a single iota of my enjoyment of these
         fleeting exceptional moments outside routine,
         repetition, pollution and the boredom of canned
         relationships.

MAN   This is because you're an exceptional woman by all
         measures. I don't know what your husband would say
         if he went back home last night. I hope he doesn't
         raise a problem.

WOMAN   If he returned, I'll not be helpless to fake up a reason
         for my absence. But I know he will not return from his
         journey before the weekend.

MAN   Still, you were extremely cautious we shouldn't meet
         at home.

WOMAN   Not out of fear he would return, but I was considerate
         of the feelings of the house itself.

MAN   Do you say the feelings of the house?

WOMAN   Yes. Houses are not merely stone. They are pulse and
         feeling, and it is decorous to take this into
         consideration, or else the relationships between us and
         the houses we inhabit would go wrong. But here, this
         open space is diametrically opposite. It is an invitation
         to liberation and freedom from all those
         considerations, provisos, fetters and conventions
         which have accumulated throughout the ages until

105

they have become walls obstructing light and air from our minds, hearts and souls.

(The man invites her to go onto the swing, saying as he swings her)

MAN My life was nothing but a dark cellar before I met you. That's why the love relationship that binds us is, to me, light and air, and after that it makes no difference whether we meet in a closed room or on naked ground blessed by the stars, because wherever you are with me becomes earthly paradise to me.

WOMAN The beauty of this relation is to be what it is, as it is now. Moments stolen from the span of routine time, moments which do not repeat themselves, as the case is with marriage relations devoid of excitement and adventure. It is a relation renewed by places, times and atmospheres. I don't want it to turn into routine which would rob it of all excitement, dazzle and variety and turn it into one of those canned, ready-made moulds into which we thrust our heads, and to which we pawn our hearts in search of comfort and security.

(She gets off the swing and goes back to gathering the luggage. In the meantime the man goes to the swings, sits on it holding an apple, which he nibbles at, his body rocking slowly with the movement of the swing.)

MAN I didn't know love, or that it has a magic touch which turns our life from one extreme to another, from boredom and resentment of life into a promise, a hope and love of life. Perhaps I would have been a drug addict or become a gangster, had I not met you at a moment blessed by heaven. The moment I set my eyes on you at The Beautiful Promise Club, I realised you were the missing part of me, without which my life wouldn't be one whole. I wish you would leave this absent husband absent forever and agree on our building a cottage on this piece of land deserted by human beings and live here for the rest of our life.

WOMAN   *(Leaves off, collecting the luggage and comes forward to sway the swing)*

I love you just as you love me and if I didn't I would not be here with you. But I don't hate my husband, home or work. I hate the routine, and I'll go back to my work and home more refreshed and more capable of overcoming the routine. It'll always be a pleasure to have this kind of meeting, once every month if you wish. This suits me better than any other arrangement.

(The man gets off the swing and pulls the bed linen off the tree branch. The woman helps him to shake, fold and put it with the other pieces of luggage on the motor cycle.)

MAN   *(As he pulls the swing)* We've got to leave before it gets hotter and there's no shade to protect us. *(He resumes his former talk)* I cannot bear to be away from you for a single hour. How can I endure our separation for a whole month? I wish I had met you one day before your marriage. Had this happened everything would have changed.

WOMAN   Don't say that, because I loved my husband when I got married to him. But who can issue a guarantee certificate to ensure that the emotions of love can remain the same, untouched by change throughout life.

MAN   I don't understand why you cannot walk out on that man to whom you aren't bound by any tie except a meaningless contract in the register of civil affairs. I'm ready to write a guarantee certificate, endorse it with my blood and make it a pledge and a covenant that my love for you will never be quenched as long as life lasts.

WOMAN   You can guarantee yourself. But I cannot guarantee myself. All I can tell you is that I'm living joyful moments with you, as it is, and I honestly wish that they continue and last. What is wrong with that?

MAN   I don't say there's anything wrong except that you're a married woman.

WOMAN   What harm does this do to you? It's my problem, and I know how to handle it. Perhaps you don't know that my husband too has his own love affairs, for the sake of which he travels and stays away from home. I quarrelled a lot with him about these relations which he denied. But I know they are there, and find an excuse for him, because I know the boredom he feels as he lives a life devoid of hobbies and variety. I do not suffer any sense of guilt for what I do. On the contrary, I feel I have reached conciliation with him and with myself. All I wish for is that our relationship keeps its secrecy and privacy, because everything will fall apart, if this relation leaks through the frame of secrecy and privacy.

MAN   I cannot bear to have one word that offends you fly in the air. That's why I shall keep the secrets of this relationship in my heart, and I'll always choose such isolated places to spend the nights of love which will bring us together till the end of life.

(They finish collecting the luggage and the other things. They stand wrapped in silence as if they do not want to leave the place.)

WOMAN   *(Pause)* Shall we really leave this place?

MAN   We leave it today to come back to it some other day.

WOMAN   I forgot to put on my shoes. Even they have become fetters. How nice it is to be free of them sometimes.

(She puts on one shoe and looks for the other, while the man gets ready to ride the motor cycle. A man's voice is heard offstage shouting.)

VOICE   Stay where you are and don't move.

(They stand looking at each other in wonder, whereas the voice resumes warning them)

Stay where you are and do not budge.

MAN   What does this fool say? What does he want from us?

WOMAN   *(Also taken by surprise)* Perhaps he is a criminal who wants to do us harm. But I don't see a weapon in his hand.

MAN   He is certainly a lunatic. *(He shouts in the direction of the voice)* Why all this shouting? Come over here and tell us what you want.

VOICE   I say stay where you are.

WOMAN   Let's leave him and go. He won't be able to overtake us.

MAN   But why does he threaten us so? *(He moves towards the voice)* Let me understand quietly. What is your objection to ...

VOICE   *(Interrupting)* Don't you hear me? I say stop. You are in danger. Any movement can cost you your life and the life of your woman.

MAN   Heavens! Where does this danger lie. *(He turns right and left.)* Please come over here and let's understand this riddle.

VOICE   Danger. I say danger. There is more than one signboard stuck all around this place saying it's dangerous. I cannot walk into this open ground because it is a mine field. A field full of mines. It has been deserted since the war. There's a mine in each inch. Do you understand?

MAN   *(Turning to the woman and exchanging a look of surprise with her)* Were we really lying down on

109

mines without knowing it?

WOMAN *(Panic-stricken)* I don't believe this. I don't want to believe what he says.

MAN *(Addressing voice)* But we walked into this place and we spent a whole night and nothing happened.

VOICE Thank heavens for this miracle. Only luck kept you alive until now. Be careful from now on. One step can finish you both off.

WOMAN Perhaps he is joking. He is lying. God! It is a catastrophe.

MAN *(Shouting)* The war ended years ago. What has kept this field full of mines? Perhaps you're joking.

VOICE I do not joke. If you want evidence, you can look behind you. Some stray horse entered this field only two days ago and a mine went off under its hooves. Perhaps you see the splinters also.

MAN *(Turning round to make sure of what the voice says)* I actually believe I see the remains of the horse, and as for the splinters, there they are scattered – nearby. Look. I see bones showing in that side also.

WOMAN I don't want to see anything. We've got to get out of here. We must get out of this place.

MAN Don't panic, my darling. Don't panic. We'll find a way out of this dilemma. *(He addresses the voice)* What is to be done now?

VOICE I don't know. I'll go notify the village police. Fortunately they are nearby. They don't have the means to help you, but they'll contact the city and ask for a solution. It will be rather difficult. Take care. Goodbye.

MAN No doubt a long time will pass before the solution

comes. I don't know how it can be. I don't know either how we can get water and food in the meantime. It may take days. And we didn't take into account except the night we spent here.

WOMAN   *(Panicking)* What do you say? Do you say days? Here? In this terrifying desert? Among these mines and explosives? Beside those bones? And under this sun which will shower us with fire in a short while? Are you out of your mind?

MAN   I wish we had a magic recipe to change us into two birds so that we can soar and escape. But we can't help it.

WOMAN   Can't you do anything?

MAN   We can do nothing but wait.

WOMAN   My throat has become dry. I want a drink of water.

MAN   We don't have any more water.

WOMAN   Then a can of juice. Anything to quench my parched throat.

MAN   *(Shakes his head sorrowfully)*

WOMAN   Have we really consumed everything?

MAN   Did we read the future to bring along extra food and drinks?

WOMAN   Then perdition inevitably awaits us. If not by the mines, then by hunger and thirst. *(She falls into his embrace, shivering)* I'm afraid. Afraid.

MAN   Always remember I'm with you. And be sure everything will end up alright.

WOMAN   I do not fear death as much as I fear scandal.

(They separate)

MAN   Forget about these dark thoughts. There'll be neither death nor scandal.

WOMAN   Don't forget I am a married woman. The scandal is no doubt coming.

MAN   We've got to think of a way out of this dilemma quickly. Perhaps we can follow the trace of the bike as it came in. *(Looks at the traces of the wheels then emits sounds of boredom)* There are many areas where the traces of the bike have disappeared. We're doomed to stay until rescue comes. It's going to be a difficult wait.

WOMAN   I don't know what the impact of the shock will be like on my husband when he gets to know about my betrayal of him. I fear also for my sick father who always takes pride in the origin of our home and our descent from an extinct royal dynasty. A piece of news like this will finish him off.

MAN   Then you're one of those in whose veins flows royal blood. This explains everything.

WOMAN   Explains what?

MAN   Explains your domineering personality and your temperament which likes variety and excitement. No wonder that the stars should select you and choose you as a friend to fondle and sing to.

WOMAN   Is this the proper time for sarcasm and joking?

MAN   What I say is neither sarcasm nor joking. I do believe that you descend from royal lineage and I'm proud of that no doubt. But the time and the place do not allow welcoming and celebrating this secret which you reveal for the first time.

WOMAN   Please, poke fun as much as you like, but don't make me the butt of your satire.

MAN It's just talk to while away the time. Don't you find this waiting difficult and boring in such a place, where nothing neighbours us except this tree.

WOMAN And those mines. Don't forget.

MAN I said the tree in the hope of recalling the primitive man when he slept among the branches of trees. That would be a lot safer.

WOMAN *(Raising her head to contemplate the branches)* Man must change into a squirrel, before he can sleep among those dead branches.

MAN Perhaps we can throw a robe on them to provide us with a shade, which can protect us from the ferocity of the sun at siesta time.

WOMAN Now you have begun to work out practical thoughts.

MAN I'm still puzzled. I don't understand what happened. We were able to get into this place and spend all this time running, playing around and moving in complete freedom, without anything happening. Then a fool comes to tell us we're walking on a field of mines and that any step we take will bring about perdition. The question is, why didn't those mines explode when we were running on them. They didn't explode, because we didn't care about them or know anything about them. We didn't take them into account, so they also didn't take us into account and left us alone. I'm sure we would have gone out safe just as we entered, if that man had not come to plant with his words the mines in our hearts.

WOMAN How stupid I was when I thought this open ground had slipped from human memory, only to discover now that human kind has never forgotten it. They have taken more care of it than any other place, because they have deposited in its depths the greatest

113

achievements of terror and perdition.

MAN   They are the traps of death, which man sets to catch another man, according to a game called war and here we're in time of peace, after long years of the end of war, and we fall in this trap. God forgive the dead ancestors.

WOMAN   I don't know why you brought us to this damn place, as if the earth lacked comfortable, safe places.

MAN   It hasn't become damn except now. You forget you were the cause. I suggested spending the night in the places you term comfortable and safe. But you wanted the taste of adventure.

WOMAN   And you have the audacity to blame me after all the sacrifices I made for your sake. I handed myself over to you and put my trust in you and what was the result? You didn't even see the signboards stuck along the road, cautioning against entering this open ground.

MAN   Wasn't it you who urged me to drive the bike at the utmost possible speed? You even wanted more than its maximum speed. How could I, then, slow down to read the signboards? You were doing this for the sake of more excitement. Why do you regret it now? Why don't you enjoy this excitement unparalleled by any excitement in the world.

WOMAN   I cannot imagine how I can stay with you for one more hour after now.

MAN   You can leave the place. Nobody is stopping you.

WOMAN   I'll go immediately. Fetch my shoe lying over there.

MAN   Perhaps it's Cinderella's shoe that'll carry you in a jiffy to the palace of your royal forefathers. How smart of you to think that if the mine goes it will hit me alone. It'll hit you too.

WOMAN   How stupid I was to overlook the happiness that filled
            my life to rush after an adventure which brought me
            humiliation and misery.

MAN   You were only using me to satisfy one of your
            caprices. Your love for me was not love but
            exploitation. It was I who was stupid when I accepted
            to be an instrument to your desires to bestow the
            element of renewal on your empty, boring life.

WOMAN   What about your life? Why do you seem mysterious
            and secretive. You don't reveal any of the secrets of
            your life and relationships. I am not that stupid or
            ignorant of your deceit, or of your relationship with
            that rich, fat and ugly widow.

MAN   And you reckon it is deceit there is another woman I
            know and meet her every now and then. I knew her
            before I knew you.

WOMAN   And did you put an end to your relationship with her,
            or do you still keep it up, with an eye on her fortune?

MAN   Now you admit you know everything about my
            relationship with her. Where is the deceit then? And if
            I did carry on my relationship with her, it was only
            because you too refuse to break off with your husband
            for my sake.

WOMAN   I've been open with you from the start.

MAN   I also was sincerely desirous to break off any other
            relationship to stay with you.

WOMAN   Do you really love her?

MAN   She loves me. I'm sure of that. And she doesn't want
            anything in the whole world except to stay with me.

WOMAN   As for you, you love nobody but yourself. You want
            me for picnicking and amusement. And you want her
            for her fortune.

MAN   Perhaps I wronged her and myself when I ran after
             your love which was nothing but mirage.

WOMAN   You can go back to her and satisfy your ambition to
             climb into the rich class.

MAN   Perhaps this is what I should do. Avail myself of the
             chance and try to float on the surface of this world
             instead of remaining at the bottom. This is what all
             people do in these times.

WOMAN   It's too late for you, my dear. You've lost me and
             you'll lose her when she gets to know about your
             deceit. You're playing a losing game.

MAN   *(pause)* What brought us here? These mines spoil
             everything.

WOMAN   You are responsible for my being here. And you've
             got to take me back where you picked me up.

MAN   Now, now? You're very optimistic, my dear. Even if
             you managed to get out of here, that will not be before
             you hear the singing of the stars for many nights to
             come.

WOMAN   What stars? Did you believe that the stars sing? That
             was nothing but a nightmare.

MAN   It was you who said that. They sing, dance, talk and
             know the secrets of men, or else astrologers wouldn't
             use them to know the future and read the unknown.
             I'm surprised. They did not tell you about the danger
             all around us. The stars have deceived you. And now
             they disappear from their sky and leave you in the
             company of terror and mines.

WOMAN   And with you, which is more cruel than the terror of
             mines. I actually want to go back home and never
             leave it or my husband. But scandal is something
             terrible. I don't know what to do with this scandal.

The police will come and the proceeding of investigations. My husband will know everything. My throat is parched. I want water. *(She picks an empty can and throws it away.)* You're the cause of all these catastrophes. Please leave me. I want to be on my own. I cannot think with you around.

MAN *(laughs sarcastically)* And where do you want me to go?

WOMAN To hell if you want.

MAN Is there a greater hell than the one which surrounds us?

WOMAN Well, I'll go then.

MAN Don't forget to close the door behind you.

WOMAN *(Rushing forward as the man tries to stop her. She takes two steps and stops frozen in her place)* I feel something moving under my foot. Help me, please. It's the mine. I need quick rescue.

MAN *(Jumps and hides in the trunk of the tree)* Don't raise your foot. Stay where you are. If you raise your foot the mine will go off. Don't move. Perhaps you imagine things. Perhaps it is not a mine but a beetle moving under your foot. Look carefully.

WOMAN It is certainly a mine. It emits a buzzing sound. Please, move. Do something. Help me before the explosion shatters my body to pieces.

MAN What can I do? I can do nothing. Stay where you are.

WOMAN Hurry up and dig a hole with your nails behind my feet. Throw yourself into it, so the mine doesn't explode in my body.

MAN My feet do not help me make any movement. Stay as you are until the police come.

117

WOMAN	*(Raises her leg without anything happening. She goes back to her place under the tree)* I was only testing your magnanimity. Come out of your hiding place, you coward. For nothing will happen, because there was no mine there.
MAN	*(Goes back to his place beside the woman)* That was joking in very bad taste. It could have been a reality, and you'd have killed yourself and me along with you.
WOMAN	And how do you want us to spend the interim. This kind of joking is useful to us, because it make us know each other more.
MAN	You know the moment of danger has its own logic, when the conscious will is absent, and nothing remains but the instinct of self-preservation.
WOMAN	What honesty the angels would envy you of! I don't know how you are not ashamed of yourself.
MAN	What do you mean?
WOMAN	I mean we're here in this place together merely because there are mines besieging us, because I do not want to see your face any more.
MAN	What a pity, for you'll see it a lot these days. Because it is the only face before you. There'll be many occasions which will make you change your feelings towards me. Come on, let the smile return to your face.
WOMAN	What? A smile becoming this ordeal. I wish I could find one drop of water, for thirst will kill me before rescue arrives.

(The man's voice is heard offstage accompanied with the clamour of a crowd of people who have come with him to watch what happened)

118

VOICE	You there!

(The man and woman stop and look in the direction of the source of voice and noise)

MAN	There he has come back. Perhaps he's brought with him the rescue team.

WOMAN	Our ordeal will be over then. Thanks to heaven.

VOICE	I have notified the police and they are still contacting the capital asking for rescue. I have with me here a number of the media men who want to talk to you.

WOMAN	My God! Look at that crowd of people. Men, women, children and cameras. They are watching us as if we were animals in a cage.

MAN	And instead of the rescue team we have the media team. No doubt they'll be overjoyed if they see a mine go off under our feet and are able to shoot it picture and sound. It'll be a world media hit.

WOMAN	It's the scandal. The unprecedented scandal. I'll be exposed before the whole world. I'm a fallen woman. This is what the world will say about me.

(She hides her face between her hands, then averts her face in the opposite direction of the source of voice before she takes her hands off her face)

ANNOUNCER'S VOICE	Would the lady please turn her face towards us for we've started shooting. Raise your voices that we can take the whole scene with picture and voice. We want some information.

MAN	*(Shouting)* We need speedy rescue. We have no water or food to enable us to wait.

ANNOUNCER'S

VOICE	We shall force the government to intervene as soon as possible. It'll be a big case which will stir public opinion and fire the spectators' imagination. Help us with information. Who are you? Where did you come from? And what are you doing in this place?
WOMAN	My God! What horrible questions.
MAN	Picnic. We've come on a picnic.
ANNOUNCER'S VOICE	I hope you've had a pleasant picnic.
WOMAN	What pleasure is he talking about? He's poking fun at us. Why don't you answer him?
ANNOUNCER'S VOICE	Did you read the signboard cautioning people against entering this place? Are you lovers who want to commit suicide in a new, original fashion which suicide lovers haven't hit upon before?
MAN	We neither saw the signboard nor read it. We didn't know it was a mine field.
WOMAN	Why don't you tell him it's he who is driving us to suicide with these silly questions.
ANNOUNCER'S VOICE	Then you were ignorant of the nature of the place. You took it for an innocent place and it turned out to be a mine field. This is the way stories always begin. All the great stories, including Man's journey through life. I'll say this in my comment. And now we want to see the lady's face. The public will sympathise with her when they see the tears in her eyes. We want to know who you are in particular, and what you do for a living.
MAN	That doesn't matter. It's beside the point. We're thirsty and we've no water. Do something to save us.

ANNOUNCER'S
VOICE   The story will be inadequate if we don't convey to the spectators Who? When? Where? How? And Why? The spectator wants to know everything. So, tell me quick who you are and what you do for a living.

WOMAN   *(To Man)* Don't tell him anything that reveals my identity.

MAN   I'm a collector working for the electricity department. I read the electricity meters.

ANNOUNCER'S
VOICE   And the lady?

MAN   *(To woman)* I'll choose for you an illusory profession. *(Loudly)* She's assistant at a perfume store.

ANNOUNCER'S
VOICE   Wonderful. Light and perfumes. What analogy and harmony! No doubt you're married.

MAN   Friends. Only friends.

ANNOUNCER'S
VOICE   Then it is an emotional adventure. We'd like to see you in a more intimate posture. That'll have a profound impression which will remain eternally in the minds of the spectators. A love scene in the middle of fire fields.

WOMAN   Tell him to leave before I look for a mine to hurl in his face.

ANNOUNCER'S
VOICE   We came here to offer you help and convey the tragedy of your presence here to public opinion.

WOMAN   It's they who are making the tragedy. They're making the scandal for us. I wish they would vanish.

121

MAN   I'm fed up. I don't know how to express my anger for
                the silliness of his talk and interrogation.

ANNOUNCER'S
VOICE   What do you want to say to public opinion?

MAN   We want to get out of this damn field as soon as
                possible. We want to go back home.

ANNOUNCER'S
VOICE   This will all happen. What else?

MAN   (To woman) What else? Shall I tell him I want to piss
                but I cannot do it with all the eyes of the cameras on
                us.

ANNOUNCER'S
VOICE   We haven't heard the voice of the lady. What do you
                want to tell your family and friends, lady.

WOMAN   He wants me to announce my scandal to the world.
                Tell him I'm dumb and do not talk. All my body has
                stiffened. I want water.

MAN   The lady is worn out. Thirst has robbed her of the
                ability to speak. I wish you could secure some water
                for us.

ANNOUNCER'S
VOICE   Could we know what you've seen and heard during
                this picnic. Anything funny that can please the
                spectators.

MAN   I wish you'd sent the national circus before you
                honoured us with your visit. That would've been a
                chance to tell you the funny things we saw and heard.

ANNOUNCER'S
VOICE   You haven't lost your sense of humour despite the
                tragedy. Still, they say that the victims of war get up
                in the night and emit voices which fill this place. Did
                you hear these voices or see their ghosts.

WOMAN	*(To man)* I don't care about the siege of the spirits or the mines. All I want is that this announcer and the photographers and inquisitive people with him disappear. We've got to expel them immediately from the place. We are not matter for a spectacle and satire. Do something, please.

MAN	*(To announcer)* No doubt we'll hear what the spirits say in the nights to come. But last night we heard nothing but the singing of the stars.

WOMAN	*(To man)* What do you say, you fool I ask you to expel them and you talk to them about the stars.

ANNOUNCER'S
VOICE   Did you say the singing of the stars?

MAN	Yes, those in the sky. Those stars we don't see now because they aren't good at the game of disguise and disappearance the way they excel in playing music and singing. They made us hear beautiful songs last night.

ANNOUNCER'S
VOICE   That'll be exciting and new. It'll be something delightful to the spectator to know the nature of this singing. Could you repeat that tune the stars sang to you.

MAN	The stars sang thus. *(He sings the same tune the woman had hummed.)*

WOMAN	Have you lost your mind?

(The man continues humming.)

ANNOUNCER'S
VOICE   Would you raise your voice that it reaches the microphone. We want you to sing loudly. Would the lady also sing with you.

123

MAN   *(To woman)* Don't be that passive. We've got to be
            hospitable to those guests who came to serve us.
            Come on, sing with me as Mr. announcer has ordered.
            We'll give them the world information hit they are
            after.

            *(He hums the tune loudly and the woman joins him.
            They sing their tune nervously, as they dance and
            convulse. They leave their place and head as they
            dance for the mine field towards the source of voice.
            Offstage rise shouts of terror, fear and warning.)*

VOICES
OFFSTAGE   Stay where you are. It's lunacy. The mines will go off
            and we too will perish with you. We appeal to you to
            stop this dance. We've no way of escape or safety. By
            God, stop. It's suicide. It's lunacy. You'll kill us all.

            *(The shouts of the group offstage rise intermingling
            with the singing of the man and the woman.)*

            *(The stage curtain closes while the shouting and the
            singing intermingle.)*

124

THE PAPER

(The scene is a drawing room and the time is morning. An old man is seated at a table in the centre of the stage, reading a newspaper. He is seated spreading the paper in front of him so that the audience cannot see his face. From time to time, he takes a sip of coffee from the cup that is on the table in front of him.

An old woman comes into the room and picks up an empty plate from the table. She is wearing a worn house dress. She is obviously the old man's wife.)

MARGARET	*(As she heads towards the door with the plate in her hand)* Did you like the dish?
JOHN	*(Without enthusiasm)* Yes, dear, it was quite good.
MARGARET	Shall I make it this way again next week?
JOHN	*(Suddenly annoyed)* Absolutely not. You know very well that regularity kills the taste of any dish, no matter how good it is.
MARGARET	*(Wistfully)* You know John, we used to have this very often in the early years of our marriage. *(Pause)* Do you remember?
JOHN	*(Sighing)* That was a long time ago. I prefer variety these days.
MARGARET	But you did enjoy it?
JOHN	*(Brusquely)* Of course I enjoyed it. I wouldn't have finished it if I didn't like it.

(Throughout this exchange, John has kept the paper in front of his face. Margaret looks ardently

at her husband, his face buried in that newspaper. Then she leaves the room, still carrying the plate.

Throughout Margaret's momentary absence, John hardly moves, except to turn to another page in a rather mechanical way. When Margaret returns, she sits down in an armchair near the fireplace, to the right of centre. She picks up some sewing and begins to chatter to John as she works.)

MARGARET   What's in today's paper, dear?

JOHN   Oh, nothing very new. It's the same old thing again, just as it was yesterday and just as it will be tomorrow.

MARGARET   But, John, why do you keep reading it if it's all the same, one day after another?

JOHN   Oh, Margaret, don't you understand? It may be the same, but it's written in a different way.

MARGARET   Is that what they call the magic of words?

JOHN   Well, I never heard it expressed in just that way, but that's precisely what I mean. Words themselves can convey a myriad of pictures. You may read about the same old thing day after day, but there's always some new revelation in the choice of words.

MARGARET   Are those who write aware of this great power they have?

JOHN   Who knows? *(Flatly)* And what does it matter?

MARGARET   I guess not very much, as long as you read it. *(She pauses, then blandly)* It's too bad you don't read me the same way.

JOHN   *(A little surprise in his voice)* What do you mean?

126

MARGARET   If I said the same thing over and over again, you wouldn't listen to me, no matter how carefully I chose my words. Now would you?

JOHN   *(Almost patronisingly)* Of course I would, Margaret. I'd listen to you if you put it in a different way each time.

MARGARET   Well, I don't possess the magic and I don't think I really want it. Somehow it would seem like witchcraft. When I was a child, whenever I heard a fairy tale, I would fancy my being a fairy, or even a witch. I imagined how marvellous it would be to have all those magical powers at my disposal. I fancied they would bring me all the happiness I might want. But now the idea doesn't appeal to me one bit. It's interesting how our desires and attitudes change.

JOHN   *(Not really understanding)* Yes, I guess it is, but you're fine just as you are, my dear. You don't need any special powers.

MARGARET   But these newspapermen do have the magical power. They bewitch their readers and make them read their articles, no matter what they contain. Isn't that the truth?

JOHN   Yes, Margaret, that is exactly right. But that's the way things have always been. Writers have always had the power to cast spells over their readers. That's what has made the publishing industry so successful.

MARGARET   *(Cynically)* And so wealthy.

JOHN   Yes, I guess you could say that, too. *(He turns to another page.)*

MARGARET   *(Looking up and staring for a moment at her husband, who seems so intent on his newspaper)* John, what section are you reading now?

127

JOHN   *(Matter-of-factly)* I'm on the entertainment section
                now. That's the fourth page.

MARGARET   Do you really find that interesting?

JOHN   I wouldn't read it if I didn't find it interesting,
                now would I?

MARGARET   *(A bit annoyed)* You needn't be so sarcastic. I was
                only asking.

JOHN   I'm sorry, dear. It's just that you sometimes ask
                such obvious questions.

MARGARET   I don't think it's so obvious at all. What in the
                world do you care about today's entertainment
                and entertainers? They're all a bunch of queers.

JOHN   Oh, I don't read about them. I'm not interested in
                that part of the news.

MARGARET   *(Angrily)* Why do you read it then?

JOHN   I want to see what's happening around town. You
                know – the shows and things like that. That part
                of the entertainment page, just as much as all
                those other stories about the entertainers.

MARGARET   Well, I don't know why you care about all that.
                You know just as well as I do that we never go out
                any more. So what difference does it make what's
                playing in the theatres around town?

JOHN   *(Indefiantly, but still hiding behind his
                newspaper)* What do you mean we never go out?
                Of course we go out.

MARGARET   *(Standing up and moving closer to him)* Is that so?
                When was the last time we went out?

JOHN   *(Calmly)* A week ago.

                                    128

MARGARET	*(She looks surprised, but continues her questioning)* And just where did we go?
JOHN	To the theatre, of course.
MARGARET	What theatre was that?
JOHN	The Old Vic.
MARGARET	And what play did we see at the Old Vic last week?
JOHN	Othello. Don't you remember, Margaret? What a poor memory you have these days.
MARGARET	*(Returning to her chair and sitting down)* Oh, John, poor John. It is you who have a poor memory. That night we saw Othello was fifteen years ago, my love.
JOHN	*(For the first time, his voice sounds disturbed)* No, it wasn't. It was last week. *(Almost panicky)* It's got to be last week.
MARGARET	*(Sadly)* Time passes very quickly, and fifteen years can sometimes seem like a week.
JOHN	But it's all so vivid in my mind. I remember every detail – when he killed his wife, smothering her with that pillow in her bed. I can see it all so clearly.
MARGARET	He regretted it afterwards.
JOHN	Yes – Yes. I haven't forgotten. It cost him his own life in the end.
MARGARET	That was a bloody period.
JOHN	And it was last week.

MARGARET   No, dear, it was fifteen years ago.

JOHN   But we do go out. I know we do.

MARGARET   No, dear. When we go 'out', it's to the park on a sunny day, and to the church on Sunday. Those are the only places we ever go.

JOHN   I don't understand how you can say that. Why, we just recently went to a party. I remember it vividly. I wore my grey morning suit and you were dressed all in white. As I recall, there were some very important people at that party.

MARGARET   (Smiling in remembrance) Yes, I remember well. There were ministers, members of Parliament, executives, and army officers. They were of the highest ranks. And everyone was smiling at us, shaking hands with us. All the famous people came, even the film stars. That was a wonderful day.

JOHN   And there were the journalists, the famous ones. They came, and I remember the flash of their cameras. It was all so dazzling, it nearly hurt my eyes. (Nostalgia in his voice) It all seems so clear, I can't believe it happened very long ago.

MARGARET   (Ignoring John's last comment) It was reported in every paper the next day. And there was our picture – you and me. Your arm was around my shoulder. That party was considered the social event of the week. That was the headline one paper used. Oh, well I remember it.

JOHN   There was champagne. I remember that, too. There was so much of it.

MARGARET   And they quoted you in the paper as saying 'this was the happiest day of your life.'

JOHN   And the best band in town played for us. Do you

remember, Margaret?

MARGARET   Oh, yes. We danced and we sang and we drank. We laughed a great deal, too. It was a lot of fun, something I shall remember for the rest of my life.

JOHN   We both enjoyed it, didn't we, dear?

MARGARET   Yes, John.

JOHN   How many days was it? Was it ten days ago – or perhaps two weeks?

MARGARET   No, dear, it was a very long time ago – many years.

JOHN   It can't be. It happened just recently. I remember every detail of it, and so do you. It couldn't have been more than a couple of weeks ago.

MARGARET   I do remember it, John. But that was when we were married. That was our wedding party.

JOHN   That's impossible ...

MARGARET   It's possible, dear. You just have a powerful sense of the speed with which the train of time passes by.

JOHN   I don't understand any of it.

MARGARET   Don't let it worry you, John. Just carry on with your entertainment section and don't let all of this spoil your enjoyment.

(There is a long pause. John continues to read his newspaper, now turning another page. Margaret finishes the first piece of her sewing, puts it aside and picks up another. As she begins, she glances momentarily at John, shakes her head with resignation, then returns to her mending.)

131

MARGARET	Tell me when you arrive at the obituary page, dear.
JOHN	It's on the sixteenth page, and I can tell you now that I shan't arrive at it in my lifetime if you keep interrupting me like this.
MARGARET	*(Smiling ironically)* Yes, dear. *(Pause)* And there isn't very much of our lives left. But I'd like to know why you want me to keep silent. Is there something you don't want me to know?
JOHN	No, Margaret, of course not.
MARGARET	Is it because I mentioned the obituary page? I just thought there must be something new there, of all places.
JOHN	Yes, dear. That's true, in a way. But it's actually the only page that's written in the same wording. It's probably the easiest page for them to write.
MARGARET	I guess it must be. But you still haven't told me why you want me to keep still. Shall I pretend we're not even seated in the same room? Or perhaps I should pretend we're strangers.
JOHN	Oh, Margaret, of course not. I don't know what's getting you so upset today. You've got me all muddled up. I have to keep reading these columns over and over again. With all this talk, I can't grasp what the writers are getting at.
MARGARET	But if it's the same thing every day, why do you have to concentrate so much? I would think you'd know the point they're driving at almost before they do.
JOHN	*(With exasperation)* Oh, Margaret ... Stop this foolishness and let me get on with my reading.
MARGARET	*(Still unable to see John's face, she looks at her*

sewing and she speaks.) What are you smiling at?

JOHN   *(A trace of fear in his voice)* I didn't smile.

MARGARET   *(Insistently)* Yes, you did.

JOHN   How could you possibly know? You can't see my face behind the newspaper.

MARGARET   I don't have to look at you to know whether or not you're smiling. I just know. I can tell by your voice. Besides, I've developed a kind of sixth sense about you through the years.

JOHN   Perhaps it wasn't a smile. Perhaps it was something else.

MARGARET   Well, then, if it wasn't a smile, what was it?

JOHN   *(After a momentary silence)* I don't know.

(Margaret looks up sympathetically towards her husband. Then she puts down her sewing, stands up, and moves towards him. When she is standing almost directly beside him, she speaks, but softly and with genuine feeling towards him. It is clear to the audience that despite some of her remarks, she is still deeply in love with the man.)

MARGARET   I am sure it was a smile, John. And I'd imagine it must have covered your entire face. *(Pause)* Ah, here you are. Your eyes are wet with tears. That happens to you after a big smile. Now tell me what made you smile, that way.

JOHN   *(Dejectedly)* I really don't know.

MARGARET   Was it a joke in the newspaper?

JOHN   *(A little afraid)* I don't know.

MARGARET   Were you dreaming?

133

JOHN	I don't know.
MARGARET	Was it a kind of nightmare?
JOHN	*(Heatedly, almost on the verge of panic)* I don't know ... I don't know ... I keep telling you I don't know ... Why do you keep badgering me this way? Leave me alone ... Just let me be ...
MARGARET	*(Softly)* John, I'm just trying to understand you. You shouldn't have smiled without letting me know what the big joke was. Now, why are you being so secretive? Just tell me why you smiled and that will be the end of all these questions.
JOHN	Perhaps – perhaps!
MARGARET	*(Interrupting)* Perhaps what?
JOHN	Perhaps I was tired.
MARGARET	Tired of what? Of reading?
JOHN	Well, yes, I guess so.
MARGARET	Then why didn't you just put down the paper? That's all you had to do if you were tired of reading it. You know, you really do make things much harder than they should be.
JOHN	I can't. *(Insistently)* You know perfectly well that I have to finish reading it.
MARGARET	*(In an understanding way)* Yes, dear, I understand. *(Pause)* Well, supposing I bring you your spectacles. That's really what you need.
JOHN	*(Resignedly)* All right.

(Margaret walks over to another table, opens a

134

drawer and pulls out a pair of large black spectacles. She brings them over to John and hands them to him. Then she returns to her chair, sits down again and picks up her sewing. John turns another page of the paper and, without even pausing, turns over another.)

MARGARET   You skipped two pages, dear. Why did you skip them? Was there something on them you didn't like? Or perhaps it was the book reviews. Am I right?

JOHN   Yes, dear, it was the book reviews.

MARGARET   You never read that, but you never told me why you don't like them. I've always been curious about that.

JOHN   That's because they never seem to be written in English. These books reviewers are never satisfied unless they can write half of every review in FRENCH.

MARGARET   I wonder why.

JOHN   Yes, I've always wondered about that myself. It's very annoying.

MARGARET   Well, no matter, the rest of the paper is quite well written. Wouldn't you say?

JOHN   Yes, I suppose so.

MARGARET   It really covers everything.

JOHN   Mm hm. I guess it does.

(There is a moment or two of silence, then the air is suddenly filled with Margaret's laughter. It becomes louder and louder, until it is nearly hysterical. At the sound, John moves his paper slightly but the audience is still unable to get a

view of his face.)

JOHN   What is it? Why are you laughing like that?

MARGARET   It's so funny ...

JOHN   What's funny?

MARGARET   *(Laughing)* Oh, John, I'm sorry. I just can't help myself. But it really strikes me funny.

JOHN   *(Impatiently)* Well, whatever it is, why don't you share it with me so I can join the laughter.

MARGARET   *(Trying to regain control of herself)* It was something that happened yesterday.

JOHN   And just what was that?

MARGARET   *(Still giggling a little)* You were holding the paper upside down.

JOHN   *(His voice filled with astonishment and fear)* What are you saying?

MARGARET   The paper was upside down and you were reading it as if it were in the right position.

(John suddenly throws the newspaper aside and stands up. He feels around the table and, in so doing, knocks the tea cup to the floor. Now the audience can see that he is a blind man. The whole discussion of the newspaper has been a sham, and a pretence for the world. But Margaret has just shattered his illusions and spoiled the masquerade.

John moves towards Margaret, leaning on the edge of the table. When he has gone as far as he can with assurance, he stops and faces towards the chair, where he knows she must be sitting.)

JOHN	That's a lie. The whole thing is a lie ... You're just saying that to humiliate me.
MARGARET	*(Ruefully)* No, John, it's true. *(Suddenly aware of John's great distress she is filled with regret for having told him the truth.)*
JOHN	You have deceived me. You have been deceiving me all this time. You should have told me. How could you let me go on holding the newspaper the wrong way? How could you be so cruel? How could you ... agh ... I can't breath ...

(John tries to loosen his tie. His fingers fumble with the knot unsuccessfully. Margaret gets up hurriedly and moves over to help him undo his tie. Then she leads him back to his chair and helps him to sit down. He is now a truly dejected man.)

MARGARET	John, I would have told you, but by the time I realised it, it was too late. You had almost finished reading it. *(Bending down to pick up the cup, she pauses. Then she places the cup and saucer back on the table.)* I'm truly sorry. I wouldn't have said anything if I'd known you were going to get so upset. I simply thought it was rather humorous incident.
JOHN	*(Strained)* Maybe it didn't happen just yesterday? Maybe I've been reading the paper upside down all these years. Who knows?
MARGARET	No, John, it happened just that once. And it was my fault.
JOHN	What do you mean by that?
MARGARET	I put the paper on the door mat a different way. I always put it down the same way, but yesterday I made a mistake. When you picked it up yesterday morning, you couldn't have known. It was all my fault, John. Please forgive me.

JOHN   *(Accusingly)* How could you make such a dreadful
                mistake?

MARGARET   Every day for fifteen years, I take the newspaper
                after you finish reading it, and I put it on the door
                mat for you to pick up and read again. I do it the
                same way day after day without a single mistake.
                Just once I put it in a different position, and you
                call it a dreadful mistake. How can you be so
                unforgiving?

JOHN   *(After a moment of self-reproach)* Are you angry
                at me?

MARGARET   *(Softly)* No, John, I'm not. *(Pause)* Are you angry
                at me?

JOHN   No, Margaret. I'm never really angry at you.
                Don't you know that.

MARGARET   *(Smiling happily)* Yes, John, I suppose I do.

                *(Margaret moves over to the side of the table,
                bends down and picks up the newspaper. She
                places it gently in John's hands.)*

JOHN   No, dear. I can't read anymore of it.

MARGARET   That's alright. You can finish it tomorrow.

JOHN   No, Margaret, that's not what I mean.

                *(Margaret frowns and looks very confused. She is
                obviously at a loss for words. Then she sees John
                slowly ripping off a page of the newspaper.)*

MARGARET   *(Confused)* John, what are you doing?

                *(John doesn't answer. He just sits there, tearing
                the newspaper, page by page, to very small
                pieces.)*

138

(Margaret watches silently and sadly. When John has finished, she walks towards him, picks up the scattered pieces, and throws them into the fire. Then she looks over at John, who is sitting there, stone-faced, hardly moving a muscle. She begins to weep but there is no reaction ...)

CURTAIN